The Sindh Police
Brief History and Developments
1947–1997

The Sindh Police
Brief History and Developments
1947–1997

AKHTAR HASSAN KHAN GORCHANI

OXFORD
UNIVERSITY PRESS

Great Clarendon Street, Oxford OX2 6DP

Oxford University Press is a department of the University of Oxford.
It furthers the University's objective of excellence in research, scholarship,
and education by publishing worldwide in

Oxford New York

Auckland Cape Town Dar es Salaam Hong Kong Karachi
Kuala Lumpur Madrid Melbourne Mexico City Nairobi
New Delhi Shanghai Taipei Toronto

with offices in

Argentina Austria Brazil Chile Czech Republic France Greece
Guatemala Hungary Italy Japan Poland Portugal Singapore
South Korea Switzerland Turkey Ukraine Vietnam

Oxford is a registered trade mark of Oxford University Press
in the UK and in certain other countries

ISBN 978-0-19-547151-9

Typeset in Minion Pro
Printed in Pakistan by
Kagzi Printers, Karachi.
Published by
Ameena Saiyid, Oxford University Press
No. 38, Sector 15, Korangi Industrial Area, PO Box 8214
Karachi-74900, Pakistan.

Contents

Preface

It has been my practice over the years to keep an account of important events in my police career along with a brief description and history of those places to which I have been posted. A study of the district gazetteer is the first thing I do when I report to a new station. In the process I have gathered some useful notes on the history of districts Muzaffargarh, Layyah, Tank (DI Khan), Jhang, Wazirabad, Multan, Lodhran, Sukkur, Jacobabad, etc. Now that the nature of police duties has undergone a major change, there is little leisure time for an officer to pursue literary activities. There is, therefore, a need to establish research centres at all district headquarters. Apart from other obvious advantages, such centres would help in improving the quality of annual administration reports, and instead of just giving crime statistics, as at present, these reports could be made more readable, analytical, and meaningful.

The golden jubilee year of Pakistan's independence (1997) persuaded me to undertake the task of compiling this book. It is by no means a research work, nor is it a very detailed or comprehensive account. Instead, I have opted to give just a bird's-eye view of the history of the Sindh Police. To keep the interest of the reader intact, I have omitted burdensome details.

I hope this booklet provides food for thought, especially to my colleagues in the police department whose valuable comments and critique would help in overcoming all shortcomings in this work.

1

A Brief History and Geography of Sindh

Sindh in south-east Pakistan forms the lower Indus basin. It is bordered to the west and north by Balochistan, Punjab to the north-east, the Indian states of Rajasthan and Gujarat to the east, and the Arabian Sea to the south. It is about 579 km long from north to south and nearly 442 km at its widest point. It covers a total area of 140,915 sq km. Dr H.T. Sorely, former Deputy Commissioner of Hyderabad, Thar Parker, Sukkur, Nawabshah, etc. recorded the total area of Sindh as 56,447 square miles (*The Sindh Gazetteer*, 1959).

Terrain

The province has a narrow coastal strip of about 150 miles in the south-west along the Arabian Sea. In the extreme west of Sindh lies a mountainous region consisting of the Kohistan section of the barren Kirthar Range. To the east is the sand belt stretching from the borders of Bahawalpur to the Rann of Kutch. Between these tracts lies the Indus Valley terminating in the deltaic region to the south-west. The northern portion of this valley is called the '*siro*' (upper), the southern the '*lar*' (lower), and in between lies the '*vicholo*' (central). These areas have rich alluvial soil and the central part has a perennial water supply from the Sukkur barrage, which together gives the province enormous agricultural potential. In the extension alluvial plains, perhaps the finest and most productive area is around Shikarpur and Larkana, comprising a 100-mile long, narrow strip running north to south, and bounded by the river Indus and the former Western Nara. Except for a small hilly tract in the south-east corner of Tharparker district (Nagar Parkar), western Sindh is the only region which is mountainous. This region is known as Kohistan. The mountains here are not high enough to catch rain-clouds during the monsoon season, with the result that the rainfall in Sindh is generally precarious. Sindh may be regarded generally as a low and flat country, with the exception of the mountains— partly limestone and sandstone—on its western boundary which also form a natural line of demarcation between this province and Balochistan.

Indus

Sindh territory was formed and is sustained by the River Indus, without which it would simply be desert. The river's length from the Kailash Range to the sea is about 1,800 miles, but it traverses Sindh for nearly a third (580–90 miles) of that distance. When snow at the river's source begins to melt in spring, and later when monsoon rains fall in its catchment areas and distributaries, the river overflows its banks. This overflow has to be contained throughout most of the river's length by bunds, although areas lying between the bunds are flooded.

Climate

Owing to its arid weather, mostly because it receives negligible rain during the monsoon, Sindh is the hottest province in the country. The average temperature in summer is 35° centigrade and a relatively high 16° in winter. But in summers, the temperature frequently rises to 45° and occasionally to as much as 50°. In the northern part of Sindh, temperature extremes are strongly marked. Jacobabad is one of the hottest places in

Pakistan, as is Sehwan, while Hyderabad, like Karachi, is generally pleasant due to the effect of the cool sea breeze.

Population

At the time of independence in 1947, the population of Sindh was estimated at 5.5 million. Since then, there have been five censuses—in 1951, 1961, 1972, 1981, and 1998. According to the 1998 census, the population of the province was almost 30 million as against a little over 19 million in 1981.

2

The Formation and Evolution of the Police

In his book, *Our Police Heritage*, N.A. Rizvi (chapter 1, p. 1) has described the police as a civic organization responsible for prevention and detection of crime and maintenance of law and order. The word 'police' appears to derive ultimately from the Greek word '*polis*' meaning '*city*' via the Latin word '*politia*' meaning 'policy'. The word was adopted into the English language in 1714 with the appointment of a 'commissioner of police for Scotland'.

Europe

Early traces of a police administration can be seen in the time of the emperor Augustus (b.63 BC), but it became an instrument of tyranny in the hands of his unworthy successors and vanished with the fall of the Roman Empire. Its renaissance is seen in the capitularies (ordinances) of Charlemagne (AD 742–814), which contain a number of regulations on the subject of police.

England

In England, the first police code was introduced in 1078 by William the Conqueror, which was more or less similar to the Norman police system in France. Prior to that, law and order was maintained by the system of 'frank-pledge.'(Frank-pledge provided for the division of each district into a series of 'tithings'. (A tithing was a grouping of ten householders living near each other who were together and collectively responsible for each other's behaviour). In 1285, King Edward I promulgated the statute of Watch and Ward aimed at maintaining peace in the city of London.

In 1585 an Act was passed for better governance of the city and the borough of Westminster, which was re-enacted in 1737 and again in 1777. The law and order situation of London in particular, and England in general, was deplorable. Crime was rampant and it was believed that in London alone 30,000 people lived by thieving and that there was one criminal to every twenty-two persons of the general population.

The dire need for an organized police force was finally acknowledged by the government and Sir Robert Peel laid the foundations for it in 1829. The British policeman is known as a 'Bobby' after him. There were srong objections to this newly-raised force initially, but its good conduct gradually overcame the opposition, especially when it was realized that crime had indeed diminished and that the police had proved to be useful. A paid country police force came into existence under the Acts of 1839 and 1840, followed by other enactments for Ireland, Scotland, and the Metropolis of London.

France

The Paris police force was created by Louis XIV in the seventeenth century. In 1697 a ministry of police was created by an Act of Directory; this was amalgamated with the Ministry of the Interior in 1852. The police were organized into two divisions: administrative and active. Not all uniformed men were employed on the streets: the 6th Central Brigade—a smart, well-dressed, and suitably equipped contingent of old soldiers nicknamed 'vaisseaux' (vessels) after the collar-badge of Paris (an ancient ship)—was formed as a large reserve force. Two central brigades controlled public carriages and another controlled the great central market. The '*bourgeois*'—police in plain clothes—dealt with detecting crime, the units that were eventually amalgamated with the '*Sureté*' watched over the morals of the capital, while the '*Brigade de Garnis*' supervised the lodging houses etc.

Arabia

In Arabia, there would have been no policing system *per se* before the advent of Islam since the tribal system itself is a system of collective responsibility. The word of the tribal chief, and tribal customs and values, were the supreme law of the land. In early Islamic society under the Prophet Muhammad (PBUH), the need for policing was not felt because every Muslim not only corrected himself but also felt responsible for stopping every next man from straying. The *Shariah* enjoins every Muslim to check the evil-doer and persuade him to repent and abstain from future commissions; thus people themselves performed the duties of the police. The momentum with which piety had taken root under the Prophet (PBUH) continued through the two and a half years' reign of the first caliph, Hazrat Abu Bakar (RA) (AD 573–634), during which time no need was felt for giving police powers to anyone. With the slackening of the initial momentum and an increase in urbanization, the second caliph, Hazrat Umar (RA), introduced night watches and patrols. The police service thus established was named '*Al-Ehdaas*'. Evidence is also available to the effect that Abu-Hurayrah, who was sent to Al-Bahrayn, was specifically given police powers (Husaini, *Arab Administration*, p. 46).

A proper police force was organized by the fourth and the last caliph, Hazrat Ali (RA), who raised a regular municipal guard named '*shurtah*', whose chief was known as '*sahibus shurtah*'. The duties of the *shurtah* included supervision of markets, checking of weights, and detection and prosecution of crime. The Umayyad kings maintained the organization but preferred to name it '*ehdaas*'. Its chief, the '*sahibul ehdaas*', also had semi-military functions: besides maintaining law and order, he also engaged rebels in battle whenever that was necessary. He not only detected and punished crime, but also removed the causes leading to it. Although policing of the provinces was left to the local governors or chiefs, the *sahibul ehdaas* also kept an eye on their police functioning.

When the Abbasids came to power, the chief police officer was given the title of '*sahibus shurtah*'. At one time, he was also the chief of the king's bodyguard and responsible for carrying out death sentences. Only a very respectable person of high status was appointed to this post. He conducted investigations and on their completion declared the *hadd*, after which the *qazi* heard the case and passed judgment. There were occasions when the *sahibus shurtah* ordered *qisas* (compensation) independently of the *qazi*.

The organization of *shurtah* underwent considerable expansion under the Muslims in Spain, where the prototype of the Mughal *kotwal* was known as '*sahibe madina*' (officer of the city) or '*sahib il lail*' (officer of the night). Policemen in Spain also came to be known as '*drabeen*' (cellars) because, in dangerous areas, they arranged armed pickets in cellars with trained dogs at the door.

Besides the *sahibus shurtah*, the Abbasids maintained another civilian officer, known as '*mohtasib*', who monitored the religious and moral activities of society. *Mohtasibs* were either honorary volunteers or paid servants of the Crown. The functions of the *mohtasib*, as outlined by Al-Mawardi (Al-Mawardi, chapter 19), included removal of beggars from the streets, stopping unqualified men from practising medicine, removing encroachments from roads, supervising behaviour towards the slaves, supervising loading of ships, and ensuring that everyone offered obligatory prayers and abstained from drinking, gambling, and other immoral acts.

Ancient India

In ancient India, policing was vested in the person of the village superintendent who may originally have been chosen by the villagers (later appointed by the kings). The *Jatakas*—stories of legendary characters written around 600 BC that relate to the nearly 550 existences through which Buddha was believed to have passed before his nirvana—throw some light on the system of self-governing village communities in the period from 600 to 326 BC. The Crown's role was to protect villages in times of war and to collect taxes in peace. The laws of Manu, recorded around 500 BC and having had a very strong influence on the political and social life of Hindus, explain the policing aspect of the king's functions, e.g. preventing violence, punishing evil-doers, maintaining patrols, fixing check posts, and appointing a number of agents or spies. The influence of the Persian and Greek systems of administrations under monarchs such as Cyrus (Kaikhusro), Darius (Dara), and Alexander, is apparent, but the successor to Chandragupta Maurya, Ashoka the Great, was under the altogether different influence of Buddhism. His Law of Piety was promulgated by means of inscriptions carved on rocks, some of which may still be seen. The Chinese travellers Fa Hien and Huien Tsang both reported on the peace and prosperity in the days of the Gupta dynasty.

Muslim India

From the eighth century onward, India gradually started coming under the sway of Islam. In AD 712 Sindh was conquered by the Arabs and the Punjab overrun by Mahmood of Ghazna, but neither put into place any Muslim institution of governance. Muslim influence on Indian administration was not felt until AD 1206, when Qutubuddin Aibak consolidated the conquests of his master, Mohammad Ghauri, with the intention of establishing a permanent kingdom. The appointment of *mohtasibs* in the department of *Al-Hisbah*, responsible for supervising the morals of the populace, seems to have been made first in the reign of Aibak's successor, Iltutmish (AD 1211–36). Balban, the ninth slave king, built roads, curbed robbery, and made the country safe, especially for highway travellers. His punishments exceeded all bounds. Mohammad, the second king of the Tughlaq dynasty (AD 1321–1414), established an admirably regulated postal system throughout the country. Feroz Shah Tughlaq (AD1351) introduced administrative reforms and suppressed the practice of mutilation and torture. He declared that he would punish all corrupt public servants as well as those who offered bribes.

The Mughals

In AD 1526, Zahiruddin Babar, the first Mughal emperor, brought the Sultanate to an end. He was preoccupied with suppressing opposition and had yet to establish a civil government when death claimed him in AD 1530. Babar's unlucky son, Humayun, had not consolidated his position when he was overthrown by Sher Shah Suri, who proved to be an exceptionally wise administrator. Sher Shah made great contributions to the growth of the civil administrative system already established under the Sultanate, and which had furnished a starting point to the Mughals. He built the Grand Trunk Road from the Indus to Bengal, along which travelling was made safe and easy as it was patrolled by police and was furnished with *serais* at frequent intervals. He also drew up a new digest of civil and penal laws. Sher Shah was as remarkable for his good sense and talent as for his justice towards his subjects. In his time, *muqaddams*, the heads of village councils, were recognized and ordered to prevent thefts and robberies. Police regulations were drawn for the first time in India, if robberies remained untraced the *muqaddams* were made to compensate the loss sustained by the victims. In his *sarkars* (districts), Sher Shah appointed chief *shiqadars* (*shiqadar-e-shiqadaran*) instead of the usual *faujdars* and empowered them to inflict heavy punishments on the lawless. He appointed chief *munsifs* (*munsif-e-munsifeen*) to watch over the conduct of *parganah* officials in order to ensure that they neither caused loss to the people nor embezzled the king's revenues. He appointed *kotwals* too, but not in unimportant places.

The political division of the Mughal Empire remained practically the same as it had been in the time of Sher Shah. Under the earlier slave kings, the provinces were known as *iqleems*, which were divided into *sarkars*. The districts were also sometimes known as *shiqs*, though in later periods the word signified subdivisions of a district. The *shiqs* comprised *khiltas* and *qasbahs*, which were also known as *parganahs*.

The Sultans of Delhi had modelled their law courts on those of the Abbasid kings of Baghdad, giving them the same functions and using the same nomenclature. They drew their inspiration for policing from the same source. However, they did not impose the Islamic system on non-Muslims, whose legal affairs were regulated according to the principles of their own faith.

A genuine desire to do good for the people sometimes prompted the Mughal kings to throw themselves recklessly into war against crime. In the summer of AD 1562, while Akbar was out hunting in Sakit, he learnt that a gang of about 4,000 brigands was infesting the neighbourhood. He gave up his sport and marched against them at the head of only about 200 horsemen, who formed his personal escort. The gang took refuge in Paraunkh, 15 miles south-east of Sakit. Regardless of the fact that he was not well supported, Akbar pressed on. He took twelve arrows in his shield and then in the chase, his elephant stumbled in a grain pit and Akbar barely escaped death. Ultimately, when the hard core of the gang had taken refuge in a building, he forced his elephant through a wall and set the building on fire. 1,000 of the brigands perished.

The severity of punishment for those proved guilty of criminal offences was awe-inspiring. Sporadic outbreaks of crime and the resulting discontent induced still heavier and more terrifying penalties, irrespective of whether they were permitted by the

Shariah. The kings often had the verdict carried out in their presence. When Adham Khan, Akbar's amir, committed a murder, Akbar personally threw him off the battlements of a fort (Sir Henry Elliot, *History of India*, iii, 618). Jehangir would have condemned prisoners pulled apart by elephants. During his reign, a dacoit with seven previous convictions was torn apart limb by limb. Shah Jehan administered poison to a corrupt *kotwal* and witnessed his death in open court. He also had a condemned man killed by snake-bite.

To further overawe criminals, executions were carried out in public. Convicts were also put to shame by being driven through public streets riding a donkey. Indefinite imprisonment until such time as a convict showed signs of repentance (*zahoor-e-asaar-e-tauba*) was awarded as a corrective measure. To make them assume greater responsibility in curbing crime, officers, including governors, were required to pay compensation to victims of untraced robberies and thefts. A Hindu merchant who was plundered was compensated from the fine realized from a police officer. Akbar encouraged just complaints against servants of the Crown and made various proclamations to this effect.

The Judicial System

The main responsibility for dispensing justice lay with the king, who tried both criminal and civil cases. In the Sultanate period, in actual practice the Sultan handled only criminal cases and only those civil cases that were of an extremely complicated nature. The Mughal emperors inspired by the example of the Umayyad and Abbasid rulers, fixed one day a week to attend personally to *mazalim* (criminal work); Akbar's day was Thursday, Jehangir's Tuesday, and Shah Jehan's and Aurangzeb's Wednesday. In his own jurisdiction, the governor of a province had responsibility similar to that of the king.

The court empowered to try cases for a group of villages or small towns was that of *qazi-e-parganah*, and for the entire *sarkar* (district) there was a *qazi-e-sarkar*. *Qazi-e-quzzat* and the Sultan (during the Sultanate period) were the appellate authorities.

The Police

In the Sultanate and Mughal periods, the chief police officer in the capital was known as the *kotwal*, corresponding to the *sahibus shurtah* of the Abbasids. The officer in charge of a *sarkar* was the *faujdar* and the officer responsible for a group of villages or *parganah* was the *shiqadar*.

The *Kotwal*

Kotwal is a Hindi word developed from the word *kote* meaning fort. The word is still used in India and Pakistan where city police stations are mostly referred to as *kotwalis*.

The *kotwal* maintained a force of *sowars* (horsemen) and *barkandazes*. He had his *chowkis* in important wards of the town, with a force of one horseman and twenty to twenty-five footmen. The *kotwal's* court was known as *chabutra*, a Hindi word meaning a raised platform for the purpose of sitting.

The *kotwal* was the official in sole charge of the town administration. His force patrolled the city at night and guarded thoroughfares. He prevented crime and investigated and reported offences. He maintained a register of local inhabitants, kept himself informed of their activities and means of livelihood, and took notice of every new arrival and departure. He also acted as a committing magistrate in cases which he considered important enough to go to higher courts.

He had to keep himself informed of all occurrences in the town and kept a strict watch over the *serais*. He prevented infanticide and forcible *suttee* and kept a watch over the houses of prostitutes and their visitors. He also prevented social abuses, a function of the *mohtasib*. He ensured legitimate disposal of heirless property, examined weights, measures, and currencies, kept an eye on bad characters, maintained peace and order, arrested thieves and robbers, supervised *rahdars* (watchmen employed in the inns), supervised transport arrangements, cleared the cities of brothels, extinguished fires, prevented distillation of alcohol, identified and located cheats, looked after customs, regulated market prices, arranged burial of unclaimed corpses, made inventories of the property of missing persons, prevented slaughter of cattle in public, kept guard over the treasury, and held charge of lockups and jails. Important government prosecutions were instituted by the *kotwal*, who was also responsible for keeping an eye on suspects whose guilt could not be proved, and on rioters.

The *kotwal* of Delhi was appointed by the king and had the additional function of master of etiquette at the royal court. *Kotwals* of provincial towns were appointed by the central government, but for smaller places they were nominated by the *subedars* or *nazims*.

Although he did not rank equal to a governor like his Abbasid predecessor the *sahibus shurtah*, the *kotwal* was a highly-respected and well-paid officer. The *kotwal* of Delhi was a man of great influence. During the Sultanate period, a commander-in-chief of the army was once given this appointment. One *kotwal* of Delhi is known to have been raised to the status of *malikul umra* (chief of the *amirs*). *Kotwals* were always selected from respectable and loyal households and this tradition was maintained to some extent even during the British period. Gangadhar Nehru, the paternal grandfather of the Indian prime minister, Jawaharlal Nehru, was the *kotwal* of Delhi prior to the 1857 war of independence. The *kotwals* were very well paid: according to one source (N.A. Rizvi, *Our Police Heritage*, p. 20), the *kotwal* of Poona received Rs 9,000 a month, although was required to maintain his men from this amount. In the Punjab, the *kotwals* of specified cities were selected and posted by the inspector-general himself, to maintain the prestige of the post. It was only recently that this authority was decentralized.

The *Faujdar*

In the earlier stages of development of human society, both in Europe and in Asia, police were only provided in cities. The rural population, till very late, was either left to itself or given small detachments of military or semi-military bodies to suppress trouble which they couldn't deal with by themselves. In Iran even today, policing is done along similar lines. Cities with a population size over a specified number are policed by a force called *shehrbani* (founder of the city), while areas outside municipal limits are looked after by the *yandarmeri* (gendarmerie), functioning under a different chief.

In Muslim India an officer known as the *faujdar* (army chief) was appointed to control crime in rural areas. The word *faujdari* is still used in Sindh for some police stations, while the code of criminal procedure is known as *zabta-e-faujdari*. While the *faujdar* looked after a district as a whole, dangerous places infested with criminals were placed under the charge of special *faujdars* who were given the necessary manpower to discharge their functions.

Faujdars were appointed by the governor in every *sarkar*. A *faujdar* divided his area into localities and the responsibility of policing each locality was fixed on its inhabitants. Thus the common man, under the guidance of *faujdars*, was being tutored in the art of living and defending himself without external help. Every village appointed its own watchmen, who were paid by the villagers and were not subjected to supervision by the state. The *faujdar* had a contingent of horsemen, but the main agency under him was of *barkandazes*. To assist him, he had *thaneders* (station-house-officers) in charge of small areas which were divided into *sarkars* and *parganahs* for the purposes of policing.

A *faujdar* was a covenanted officer. He was empowered to take help from neighbouring *faujdars* in time of need and to try petty criminal cases; appeals against his orders were made to the governor. In cases of untraced thefts and robberies, the *faujdar*, like the *kotwal*, was required to pay compensation to the aggrieved persons.

The *Shiqadar*

In smaller towns, the *shiqadar* was a prototype of the *kotwal* and had petty magisterial powers. He was mainly a revenue officer but was also required to assist in the prevention of crime. In a *parganah*, the *shiqadar* represented both the *kotwal's* magisterial functions and the general executive and police functions of the *faujdar*. An appeal against the *shiqadar's* order was made to the *kotwal* in the first instance, then to the governor and finally to the king.

The East India Company

With the decline of the Mughal Empire, the East India Company emerged as the rising power in the subcontinent. By that time it had established its factories in Surat, Calicut, Masaulipatam, etc. Madras and Bombay were established as factory-towns with their supervisors as presidents, whence the name 'presidencies'. They were units in themselves and had contingents of traders, soldiers, writers, book-keepers and peons, all working under the president.

In Madras, the first Police Regulation was passed in 1802, followed by another in 1812, and in 1834 a deputy superintendent of police was appointed. In 1854 the court of directors of the East India Company felt that the police should be placed under the direction and control of a district superintendent of police.

Police enactment in Bombay, of which Sindh long formed a part, began in 1818 and continued until 1833, investing land-holders and others with police powers, while the superintendence of police remained with the *faujdari adawlat* (criminal court). Drawing inspiration from Charles Napier's police organization in Sindh, the Bombay police was remodelled in 1853. It was made an autonomous unit with a superintendent of police in every district, who was generally subordinate to the district magistrate but had extensive control over his force, and a police officer for every *tehsil* in a similar relationship with the *mamlatdar* (*tehsildar*). Supreme control of the police was transferred from the *faujdari adawlat* to the government, but when it was found that the judicial secretary had neither the time nor the know-how, in 1855 it was transferred to a new officer, designated commissioner of police, who was also made inspector of prisons.

The police organizations of Bengal, the Punjab, and other provinces were in the process of evolution but for the sake of brevity, they have not been included in this narrative.

3

Emergence of the Sindh Police

The author of the *The Sindh Gazetteer*, Dr H.T. Sorley, has given a very comprehensive account of the emergence of Sindh police. In the days of the Talpurs, the administration of the country was entrusted to *kardars* who were in charge of different districts and were both revenue and judicial officers. They administered the *Shariah* as interpreted by accredited doctrines. The Mirs were not cruel and had an aversion to capital punishment. Mutilation was the penalty for the worst crimes and was often commuted to prolonged imprisonment for the privileged classes. Other punishments were imposition of fines, shaving off of the beard, blackening of the face, flogging, and confinement in the stocks. There were no organized jails, nor was any provision made for the subsistence of prisoners; that was the concern of their relatives or the charitable public. Trial by ordeal was allowed. The unwritten law of the Baloch which allows the husband to kill his wife for infidelity prevailed generally. The police department consisted of a few miserable *sowars*, and only in the major towns. But in a society where every man carried arms to defend and avenge himself, a police force was superfluous.

They had an excellent system for the detection of crime, the abolition of which under the British rule was regretted by many officers. The liability for all stolen property rested on the village or estate in which the theft occurred until the footprints of the thief were traced to another, in which case the liability was transferred to that village or estate. Thus it was in the interest of every *zamindar* (landlord) to see that he harboured no thief within the limits of his estate. Capital sentences were decided by the Mirs in person, as were appeals against the decisions of their *kardars* in cases judged by them. It was a general condition that both the plaintiff and the defendant had to pay a high sum of money for a hearing, and still more for a verdict.

An organized police service was introduced in the province for the first time by the British. The duties of the police were entrusted by the Mirs to the *kardars* and *jagirdars*, under whom watchmen were employed to guard the town gates by day and to patrol by night, while villages had their own watchmen and trackers who were paid at harvest time like other village servants. In Hyderabad, a *kotwal* or city magistrate with police powers and a force of twenty peons was employed; their remuneration, like that of all the Ameer's establishments, consisted partly of perquisites. In the country, an unwritten law held every *zamindar* answerable for any criminal tracked into his limits until he was tracked out again. This system, reinforced by the prompt and stern punishments then in vogue, was very effective, and there is evidence that the introduction of British methods was followed by a notable increase in ordinary crime.

Early Development of the Sindh Police

A system of military police was introduced by Sir Charles Napier after the conquest of Sindh in 1843. Not wishing to bring his army into close contact with the people, Napier organized a force of 2,400 armed police under military officers and apparently quite independent of the Collector. Napier's system was regarded as the model for most of what was good in subsequent reforms of the Indian police, and it has undergone less change than any other branch of his administration. The two cardinal principles of this system were that (1) a police officer should be independent of the magistracy, and (2) that he should exercise no magisterial functions.

The Sindh police force was modelled on the pattern of the Royal Irish Constabulary. It was commanded by an officer who was given the title 'Captain of Police' and assisted by three lieutenants, one each in Karachi, Hyderabad, and Shikarpur. Jacobabad and Thar Parkar were administered as political agencies and headed by army officers. The first lieutenant of the Karachi police was Lieutenant Edward Charles Marston, while the first magistrate of Karachi was Captain Preedy.

On 23 March 1843, on Napier's orders, Lieutenant Marston, then staff officer to the First Brigade, proceeded to Karachi to establish a police force. He looked scarcely eighteen years of age when he moved to take command of the police. Captain Preedy reported (Aftab Nabi, PSP, reported speech, 2000) that the police force consisted of 190 mounted men, 130 rural foot constables, and nineteen city police detectives, with a reasonable proportion of native officers. They were armed with swords and matchlocks and performed duties as watchmen, night patrols, and guards. The police also had trackers whose duties were purely detective and who were selected for their intelligence from amongst the best *puggies* or foot-trackers of Sindh. Captain Preedy also mentioned that the mounted police were very unpopular amongst the residents of Karachi, who constantly complained of their hectoring and overbearing conduct. An idea of fear the mounted and armed police inspired can be had from the fact that when, in September 1843, a tribal chief organized a robbery in the suburbs of Karachi which also resulted in murder, the arrested accused admitted that their chief had ordered them to commit the crime and the tribe delivered him to the police. The chief was tried along with his two companions and hanged in the presence of Marston and a few policemen, sixty miles away from the nearest army soldier.

To sustain the rural police, an irregular cavalry was created which gave the police confidence and courage. Napier's recruitment of personnel suited colonial priorities. He selected persons who themselves or whose families had suffered cruelty at the hands of the erstwhile rulers and who thus hated their masters. Captain Rathborne, the magistrate of Hyderabad in 1845, believed that the police also conducted espionage. It was this secret police which the explorer Richard Burton mentioned in one of his books in 1877.

The police helped magistrates in finding carriages and means of transport, sometimes ensured provision of forced labour, and were also responsible for the supervision of jails. In Karachi, persons found on the roads during the night were stopped by the police and brought before the authorities—Preedy had specifically ordered that any one moving on the roads after 11 p.m. was to be apprehended.

On 6 February 1844, Napier issued an order forbidding the carrying of arms. (Aftab Nabi, PSP, reported speech, 2000). Some exceptions were made, but only for those tribal chiefs who had submitted before the colonial authority. Police recruitment policy was based on colonial expediencies, so such persons were often inducted in order to ensure their continued loyalty.

Edward Charles Marston retired from the police in 1869 but continued to serve in the army, finally retiring in 1878 with the rank of major-general. In a period of twenty-five years (1843–68), Marston had transformed a mass of irregular manpower in Karachi into a very effective police force which was cited all over India as a prime example of how to attain colonial aims. Eventually, in the latter half of the nineteenth century, police forces all across the British Empire were modelled along the lines of the Karachi police (Aftab Nabi, PSP, reported speech, 2000).

Command

The command of the Sindh police was entrusted to a military officer who functioned as the captain of police and under whom three lieutenants of police, also military officers, controlled the district forces of Karachi, Hyderabad, and Shikarpur. The second captain of the Sindh police, Lieutenant E.C. Marston, had saved Napier's life during the Battle of Miani. He served until the post was abolished. Later a general, Marston became a well-known figure at the Karachi racecourse until his death in 1902, about fifty-nine years after the conquest of Sindh.

In 1861 the designation of 'captain' was altered to 'commandant', with lieutenants appointed as captains of police. In 1865, when the posts of commandant and captain were abolished, command of the police devolved upon the Commissioner of Sindh, and district forces were placed under superintendents. In 1905 the Commissioner's responsibilities concerning the equipment, discipline, and efficiency of the force were transferred to a deputy inspector-general of police for Sindh.

The general structure of the Indian police force was set out in the legislation of 1861, which provided for a provincialized police that was to be administered by local government, not subject to the control of the Governor-General. Under the system now in force, the district superintendent of police is subject to dual control—the force he commands is subject to the general control of the district magistrate for the enforcement of law and maintenance of order in the district, while the working and efficiency of the force is governed by a departmental hierarchy comprising a deputy inspector-general and an inspector-general. Generally speaking, the superintendents of police deal with the district magistrates on judicial and magisterial matters and with their departmental chiefs on the internal working of the force.

The Curzon Police Commission of 1902/3 modernized police working by providing for the direct enlistment and training of educated Indians as police station officers, and by creating specialized police agencies under each local government for the investigation of specialist and professional crime. This was the genesis of the criminal investigation department, which was placed under a deputy inspector-general. There also came into being an intelligence bureau, under the home department of the government of India, which collected information from all provincial criminal investigation departments and worked out inter-provincial liaison.

District Police Headquarters

In the present-day organization there is a superintendent of police with a headquarters (police lines and parade ground) in every major town of a district. All clothing, arms, ammunition, and accoutrements are stored here for provisioning police stations and outposts of the district. Constabulary recruits, enlisted by the superintendent, are taught drill and departmental duties here and, on successfully completing training, are posted out to fill vacancies. The headquarter lines also have armed police who mount guard on treasuries in the district and provide prisoner and treasury escort. The armament of the police has been modernized, their main weapons now being the .410 bore musket and the .303 rifle. At most headquarters there is also a reserve of armed police, and in larger towns, a police station and station house officer (*thana* and *thanedar*).

Police Station

It is at the police station where the public comes into most contact with the police and vice versa. Whether in a large city or in a *mofussil* (rural area), the *thana* is the place where people go with their troubles and grievances. In dealing with such callers the *thanedar* (SHO), like police of all ranks, is supposed to be always on duty, and is chiefly guided by the fourteenth chapter of the Code of Criminal Procedure and the Second Schedule of that Code. This Schedule lists nearly all the penal offences and specifies whether or not they are cognizable by the police (see p. 26).

Chapter 14 lays down that cognizable complaints must be instantly recorded, visited, and investigated. A non-cognizable complaint is merely noted in a separate book, but to seek redress the complainant must approach the court. The complainant, in a cognizable case, has his complaint not only recorded, but also investigated without payment of a fee. If the *thanedar* establishes a *prima facie* case against the accused, the prosecution in court is conducted free of charge by a public prosecutor, who is an officer of the police service.

When the Police Commission in 1860 devised a policy for the police—one that remains valid even today—they laid down two criteria for determining the number of policemen required for every district, i.e. (1) one policeman per every square mile, and (2) one policeman per every thousand of population. In towns it is well enough to have the available police concentrated at the police station, but in the *mofussil* the *thana* could very often be as much as fifty miles from the extreme limits of its jurisdiction. In such cases it is profitable to detach a portion of the police station's strength under a head-constable to man an outpost where complaints can be received and investigated without the injured party having to undertake a long journey. Police functions are more effectively discharged if the force is widely dispersed within its area of jurisdiction.

A directly recruited candidate who comes in through the Police Training School as a *thanedar* is a graduate and can rise to be an inspector or a deputy superintendent (DSP) and, in exceptional cases, even a superintendent (SP). The directly recruited DSP has a good chance of becoming an SP and perhaps a deputy inspector-general (DIG). Those who join as assistant superintendents (ASPs) can be assured of promotion to the rank of SP, and they qualify for consideration for further promotion to the rank of DIG after twenty-five years service. All ranks must serve for a period of thirty years to earn a full pension. During British rule, members of the police force were eligible for the award of the King's Police Medal or the Indian Police Medal for long and meritorious service for conspicuous gallantry.

4

Current Organization of
the Sindh Police

The police in Pakistan are provincially administered as law and order is entirely a provincial subject. Each of the four provinces of Pakistan has a certain number of administrative divisions—Punjab has eight, for example, and Sindh has five—and every division consists of four or five districts. The chief of police of the province is the inspector-general (IG) who is responsible for the maintenance of law and order and is accountable to the chief executive (chief minister) through his administrative departmental head, i.e., the home secretary. The IG is assisted by two additional inspectors-general (Additional IG Sindh Police and Additional IG Special Branch) and a number of DIGs. The organization tree as on 14 August 1997 and in 1947 may be seen at Appendices 1 and 2.

The IG's headquarter is the Central Police Office (CPO) where a number of Assistant Inspectors General of the rank of SSP look after various branches on behalf of the IG (see App. 1).

DIG (Headquarter) supervises the working of all the AIGs whereas DIG (Crimes) deals with the crime situation and statistics, and supervises the investigation of cases especially entrusted to the crimes branch by the IG. DIG (Traffic) supervises the performance of the traffic superintendents (SPs) and assists the IG on matters related to traffic. DIG T&T (Technical and Transport) deals with telecommunications and motor transport and is responsible for the overall supervision and maintenance of the fleet of 2,664 vehicles. Transport and telecommunications stores are also procured through him. DIG T&I (Training and

PRIME MINISTER

نمبرایف۔۔ (۲۸)ای ایس ٹو (۲)ای ٹی/۹۹
مورخہ ۲۹ مئی ۱۹۹۹

محترم جناب گورچانی صاحب'
السلام علیکم ورحمۃ اللہ وبرکاتہ!

مجھے یہ جان کر بے حد خوشی ہوئی کہ گولرو سے پی آئی اے کے ہوکر طیارے کے اغوا کو خوش
اسلوبی کے ساتھ ناکام بنا دیا گیا۔ طیارے کے علاوہ مسافروں اور عملے کے ارکان کی بحفاظت رہائی جہاں
پوری قوم کیلئے باعث فخرو اطمینان ہے وہاں آپ کی مستعدی' مہارت اور حاضر دماغی کا مظہر بھی ہے۔
آپ نے جس پیشہ ورانہ انداز میں اپنی جان کی پروا کئے بغیر بھائی جیک تک کو روکتے ہیں مدد دی وہ جذبہ
قابل تقلید و تحسین ہے۔ میں آپ کے خلوص اور جذبہ حب الوطنی کی تہہ دل سے قدر کرتا ہوں اور
توقع رکھتا ہوں کہ ملک و قوم کو جب بھی آپ کی ضرورت پڑی تو انشاء اللہ آپ لبیک کہیں گے۔

نیک تمناؤں کے ساتھ
والسلام
آپ کا مخلص
نواز سرشریف
(محمد نواز شریف)

جناب اختر حسین گورچانی
ایس ایس پی
حیدرآباد

Prime Minister's letter of appreciation to the author as SSP

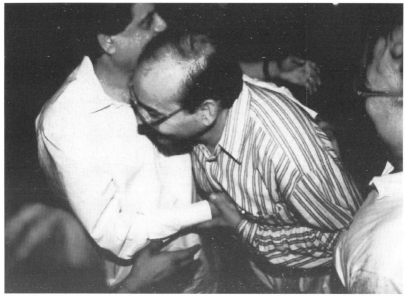

The author greets former Chief Minister of Sindh Abdullah Shah

Sindh Police action reported in the Sindhi daily *Kawish* dated 27.5.1998 and other daily newspapers.

Officers of Jacobabad police, in December 1997

Meeting of the Hindu *panchayat* (council) to appreciate the efforts of the administration in recovering three Hindu boys from dacoits

SSP & DC, Thatta briefing the media about recovery of a hostage

Author's farewell as SSP, Sukkur at Circuit House

DSP HQ, Thatta presenting an *ajrak* and a *topi* to the author

Map of Sindh

ASP's in training at the National Police Academy

A Police Armoured
Personnel Carrier

Police Commandos

Elite Course Training

Providing security for the Muharram processions

The author with Shafiq Khosa, Commissioner; Mushtaq Shah, DIG; and Suhail Shah, DC discussing measures for maintaining law and order

Inspection of Police Lines, Hyderabad

Quarter-Guard

Inspections) supervises the working of training institutions, i.e., the Police Training Schools Shahdadpur, Larkana, Khairpur, Saeedabad, ATT Metroville Razzakabad, etc. The principals of these institutions are police officers of the rank of superintendent.

DIG (SRP & Security) is the commandant of the Sindh Reserve Police (SRP)—a strike force of 9,000 officers and men which comes to the aid of the district police whenever required by the latter for maintenance of law and order, riot control, security of VIPs and vital installations, etc. He also supervises the working of SPs (SRP) Karachi, Hyderabad, and Sukkur.

Additional IG (Special Branch) is responsible for providing advance intelligence to the IG on activities such as political or religious meetings, sectarian strife, labour unrest, disturbance of law and order including terrorism, etc. He is assisted by SPs (Special Branch) located in Karachi, Hyderabad, and Sukkur.

The Divisional and District Organization

The divisional and district organizations play a vital role in police functioning. The DIG in charge of a division is a supervising officer who monitors the working of his deputy superintendents of police (DSPs) or, in the case of larger districts like Hyderabad, Sukkur, Larkana, and all the five districts of Karachi, senior superintendents of police (SSPs). A DIG is an officer of Grade 20, SSP of Grade 19, and an SP of Grade 18.

A district SP is the officer who is directly responsible for the maintenance of law and order in the district. He has to liaise with the district magistrate and, now that the judiciary is being gradually separated from the executive, with the session judge on matters relating to criminal justice. For inter-departmental issues, he is answerable to the DIG, who evaluates his performance by initiating his annual confidential report (ACR).

For the purpose of police administration, a district is divided into three, four, or even more sub-divisions, each headed by an officer of the rank of DSP or ASP. Each sub-division consists of a certain number of police stations, which are the primary unit in the system of criminal justice. The station house officer (SHO) is an officer of the rank of either sub-inspector (SI) or inspector who exercises vast powers conferred upon him under the Code of Criminal Procedure. A police station covers a number of *dehs* (villages) or revenue estates and a defined area which is duly notified by the provincial government. A crime committed in a certain village is reported to and investigated by the police station in whose jurisdiction the village falls.

According to the Pakistan Penal Code, which is derived from the Indian Penal Code, crimes fall into two categories: cognizable and non-cognizable. Cognizable crimes are those in which the police must intervene by registering the case in the First Information Report (FIR) register of the police station. The SHO either investigates the case himself or entrusts it to one of his subordinates, i.e., an SI or an assistant sub-inspector (ASI). The investigating officer (IO) collects all the available evidence, arrests the accused person or persons, and submits a complete challan of the case to the court of the magistrate, civil judge, or session judge of the area—or, if as a result of the investigation the charges are not proved, it is the IO who recommends that the case be dropped. Non-cognizable crimes are a set of offences which are of a relatively mild nature. Although such offences are punishable under law, the police do not take cognizance of these cases and hence do not intervene. In such cases, the complainant has to file a suit in the court of the area magistrate or judge, who decides the case by way of summary proceedings. Besides performing crime-detection duties, the SHO also provides security to VIPs visiting the area of his police station and to vital installations, mans picket duties and *nakabandi* points, and carries out night patrolling in his area.

Maintaining the record of a police station is the duty of a head constable who is commonly known as *munshi* or *moharrir* (station clerk). He is assisted by one or two constables.

Besides having a chain of police stations under command, a district SP also has a system of regulating traffic through traffic sergeants. Sub-divisional police officers (SDPOs) are only responsible for the functioning of police stations while a designated DSP or ASP (HQ)—or even an Additional SP (in larger districts)—supervise the working of traffic sergeants, as also of the driving licence branch and police lines or police HQ, where a reserve inspector (RI) or lines officer is in charge. A district armed reserve is kept standby in the police lines for emergencies. Arms, ammunition, tear-gas equipment, clothing, and other stores are maintained in the police lines. The motor transport officer (MTO), normally an ASI or an SI, is responsible for the upkeep of the police vehicles in the district.

Intelligence gathering is the responsibility of a separate branch which functions under an inspector or an SI. It is known as the 'Security Branch' in the Punjab and DIB (District Intelligence Branch) in Sindh. In prosecuting cases challaned in the courts, the SP is assisted by a prosecuting deputy-superintendent of police (PDSP), who also scrutinizes all the cases before submitting them to the courts.

Matters relating to transfers, postings, recruitment, etc. are looked after by an orderly assistant sub-inspector (OASI) in the Punjab and by a sheet clerk in Sindh. The office is run by an office superintendent along with assistants, accountants, senior clerks, junior clerks, etc.

5

Police Working before 1947

The Sindh police was a fully established force by the beginning of the twentieth century, but an analytical study of its working since then till 1947—a period of almost half a century—shows that it was a time of great difficulty from the police point of view. It included two World Wars, with heavy retrenchment following the end of the First World War, a long period of depression in the 1920s and 30s, and from then onward a sharp increase in political agitation and communal tension that often resulted in civil unrest and serious outbreaks of violence. These decades also saw the confusion consequent to Partition and the emergence of Pakistan. Frequent constitutional changes after 1947 disrupted established systems of administration, giving rise to additional problems. After Partition, when for several years there were shortages of food and other essential items, the problem of smuggling assumed formidable proportions. These and other black-marketing offences—which stemmed from a system of controls that were a prevalent feature of the economy from the beginning of the Second World War onwards—further increased the burden imposed upon the police.

While it is generally believed that the colonial era in Karachi and Sindh was one of effective crime control, the annual police reports and memoirs of officers of that time indicate that the situation was not so satisfactory. In and around Karachi, the major problems were burglary, theft, highway robberies, cattle theft and *karo-kari* or *siah-kari* (honour killings). Despite all efforts of the colonial government, Karachi in the latter half of the nineteenth century was not a safe place. The comments of the then commissioner Sindh, incorporated in the annual police reports, emphasize that controlling crime was always very difficult and much depended on the support, information, and co-operation of the tribal chiefs (Aftab Nabi, PSP, reported speech, 2000).

After the middle of the nineteenth century, cattle theft became such a major problem that an ICS officer, Mr Taunton, was appointed chairman of a committee to enquire into the crime of cattle-stealing in Sindh. While this may not have been a major problem in the town of Karachi itself, the outskirts were always prone to it. Initially Charles Napier, who resorted to severe punishments including hanging to curb crime, tackled the practice of *karo-kari* very vigorously. In spite of this, the problem continued during the entire period of British rule in Sindh, and the government was not effective in controlling this heinous crime.

In the last decade of the nineteenth century, the police were confronted with two major problems. In rural Sindh, especially areas now forming part of Sanghar, Mirpurkhas, Khairpur, etc. the Hur rebellion assumed very serious proportions. It was finally put down by hanging Bachu Badshah and by incarcerating Hurs along with their families in concentration camps set up at various places in areas now forming Mirpurkhas division. Meanwhile, the urban areas, especially Karachi, were in the grip of a plague, and much time, energy, and manpower of the Karachi police was devoted to duties related to the epidemic. In the first two decades of the twentieth century the Karachi police were busy re-organizing and re-structuring, although some of the innovations led to disastrous results. In the 1930s and 1940s the Karachi police and the CID were fully occupied in trying to detect subversive literature and control bomb blasts organized by some extremist Hindu parties. This period also saw rising tensions between Hindus and Muslims in Karachi that culminated in the 1935 riots in Shershah and Mevashah areas. A battalion of the Royal Sussex Rifles resorted to firing, killing more than thirty-six people. Despite stiff protests, including speeches in the Legislative Assembly, the colonial government did not even order an enquiry.

All along, the attitude and style of the police were those of colonial masters rather than public servants. The police strength was nominal, but because it was held in great fear and awe it maintained strict law and order and dealt with violations with an iron hand. This was the situation in the mid 1940s.

The 1920s

Some brief extracts from Police Administration Reports of this period will give a fair idea of the nature of the problem of law and order which prevailed in Sindh and Khairpur State, and the manner in which the police dealt with these problems. In the Police Administration Report for 1924, it is stated:

> The population of the province, according to the census of 1921, is 3,279,377, with the total of true crime standing at 9,047, the proportion of true crime works out to a highest ratio, shown again by Karachi headquarters, as 1 to 907. The proportion of true crime to police works out at 3.1 offences to 1 policeman, exclusive of the armed and some of the mounted police whose ordinary duties are not connected with crime investigation, and of cognizable crime investigated, to 3.88. The proportion of population of each policeman is 623 men. (*Sindh Gazetteer*, p. 711).

Statement showing incidence (1924) by districts per 1,000 of the population of cognizable crime etc.

District	Cognizable crime reported	Murder	Attempts at murder and culpable homicide	Dacoities	Robberies	House-breaking with intent to commit an offence	Thefts including cattle thefts	Cases of receiving stolen property
Karachi Headquarters	9.61	0.04			0.11	1.54	4.30	0.22
Karachi District	2.94	0.05	.01	0.02	0.04	0.57	1.57	0.10
Hyderabad	2.57	0.05	.02	0.002	0.01	0.62	0.95	0.12
Sukkur	4.09	0.06	.03	0.03	0.05	1.36	1.29	0.07

Larkana	3.47	0.07	.05	0.02	0.07	1.10	1.03	0.13
Tharparker	1.86	0.03	.02	.0605	0.02	0.32	0.88	0.05
Upper Sindh Frontier	2.86	0.20	.09	0.02	0.02	0.53	1.07	0.11
Nawabshah	2.50	0.08	.05	0.01	0.04	0.62	1.04	0.10
Total	3.61	0.06	.63	0.01	0.04	0.85	1.47	0.12

The Report further remarks that:

> ...on looking at the previous report for 1923, it will be seen that the proportion of reported crime per 1000 of the population is higher in Sindh than in any other province, except Burma, which has 4.15. The next lowest is the Central Provinces with 2.81 as compared with Sindh's 3.61. Then as regards crime per policeman, Sindh heads the list with 2.58. The Central Provinces coming next with 3.64 and Bombay very low down the list with 2.58. Sindh has 9.55 sq. miles per policeman as compared with 2.66 in the Northern Division, 5.58 in the Central Division and 6.01 in the Southern Division of the Bombay Presidency. As regards crime per policeman, Sindh is again a very bad last with 2.28 crimes. The Northern Division has 1.28.

The comments of the deputy inspector-general of police on this are: 'I think from the above figures it will be admitted that Sindh is very much under-policed or the presidency over-policed and a request for an increase is not unreasonable.'

As regards cattle theft, the Administration Report of the same year states:

> This of course has again been the outstanding feature of the year's crime. The average Sindhi policeman would not know what to do were this not the case. Before each wave of repressive action, cattle theft recedes only to return to its original position, and demands of the efficient Police Station Officer endless effort and endless optimism. In my report last year, after commenting on exemplary punishment for cattle theft, I made the following remarks which I venture to repeat. 'The whole question of cattle theft turns on the facilities of report to the police and trial in the courts. The cattle thief abounds because losers of cattle rarely report their loss to the police.

A loser of cattle does not report to the police because (1) the police post is distant, (2) the machinery of the courts takes so long to operate that he is involved in endless inconvenience and considerable expense before the property recovered by the police is restored to him. He naturally prefers to take the easy way out of it all and pay his 'Bhung' and to recover his property. The existence of 'Bhung' is clear proof of the inadequacy of the law. The location of additional police posts would remove the first disability from which the complainant suffers; proof of this, if it be wanted, lies in the increased support of crime from any area in which a police post is newly established. But even the location of a police post will only benefit a tithe of the actual sufferers; the remainder would prefer to cut their losses because of the waste in journeys endlessly repeated to and from the courts'.

On the question of the criminal tribes in Sindh, the commissioner in Sindh in his report of 30 April 1926 remarks:

The report of the Deputy Inspector-General of Police is fairly satisfactory so far as it goes, as it shows that the Hurs have behaved well during the year, while the Jagiranis have not shown any tendency to revert to the criminal habits which they have given up, at least for the time being. But it is obvious that we are present only on the fringe of the subject and that no real effort is at present in action either to prevent the activities of criminal sections of the population as a whole, or to reform the small proportion of those sections which are under observation (*Sindh Gazetteer*, p. 712)

The steady pattern of crime is shown clearly by the number of offences under the Indian Penal Code recorded for the years 1923, 1924, 1925, and 1926 (Ibid., p. 713).

Offences under the Indian Penal Code	1923	1924	1925	Triennial Average	1926
Murders	175	173	158	169	186
Attempts at murder and culpable homicide	127	85	108	107	88
Dacoities	19	27	22	23	21

Robberies	101	89	100	97	77
Housebreaking with intent to commit an offence	2,990	2,546	2,659	2,732	2,589
Thefts (including cattle thefts)	4,010	3,969	3,612	3,864	3,628
Receiving stolen property	412	306	360	359	411

The police have always been concerned about the number of undetected cases and also about the percentage of cases which fail to end in conviction. In the year 1926 the number of real cases under the Indian Penal Code increased from 8,119 to 8,384, and the percentage of undetected cases dropped from 50.12 to 47.26. The percentage of cases ending in conviction fell from 76.45 to 68.28, which is certainly not satisfactory. The percentage of stolen property recovered fell from 37.05 to 32.00. Property valued at Rs 693,623 was stolen in 1926 as against Rs 672,466 in 1925. The percentage of persons arrested by the police and convicted, to persons tried, fell from 46.44 to 43.54 which was the lowest figure for the quinquennium commencing 1922. As regards magistrates' cases, the percentage of persons convicted to persons tried dropped from 17.83 to 16.99. These results in the Commissioner's opinion can be regarded only as unsatisfactory. In the Sessions Courts better results were obtained; the percentage of convictions to cases tried increased from 66.33 per cent to 69.28 per cent. (Ibid., p. 713).

In the 1927 Police Administration Report, the district superintendent of police, Upper Sindh Frontier, an area to which the Sindh Frontier Regulations applied, remarked:

The Baloch has changed his views very much. Many cases have come to my notice in which innocent women have been murdered. Avarice and escape from heavy punishment are easily satisfied merely by declaring their wife *Kari* with no substantial proof to support the charge. Discouragement of this barbarous practice is called for. It can only be obtained by the infliction of heavier punishment and a considerable decrease in the amount of compensation awarded is necessary, for as long as a dead woman is worth a considerable amount of money, whereas alive she is valueless, we shall have dead women. (Ibid., p. 714).

1930–47

1930 was a particularly difficult year for the police. The commissioner considered that the outstanding feature of the year was the loyalty and devotion of the police force in the face of very trying circumstances. In the first half of the year the Pir of Kingri, the spiritual leader of the Hurs and highly esteemed by all Muslims was arrested. In the second half of the year the civil disobedience campaign, preaching as it did contempt for authority, put the police in a very awkward position; they were subjected to constant abuse and ridicule, particularly in Karachi. Not only did the police force hold fast, but throughout maintained a very fine standard of discipline. Disorders in Sukkur that year took a very serious turn. When the annual floods were at their peak, a communal riot broke out in Sukkur and continued intermittently for three days, resulting in the death, of thirty people and injury to two hundred. An attempt by some *banias* (members of a Hindu caste) in a political procession to hold up a Muslim *tongawala* started the riot. The *banias* fled in large numbers from Sukkur and took refuge in different parts of the district. Then a rumour spread that the *sarkar* (government) had ordered Muslims to loot the *banias*. This appealed to the credulous rustics. Looting started in the rural areas and within a week spread to five *talukas*. The police forces were reinforced by British and Indian infantry, but sporadic looting continued till 16 September. The police operated for over two months under the most trying conditions during the peak of the upper Sindh hot weather to protect the *banias* from the consequences of their own political activities. Throughout the operation the district superintendent of police, Mr Ray, displayed extraordinary energy and resource. Twenty murders and over three hundred dacoities were recorded.

During the same year, cattle thieving proved a greater menace than ever. In the Upper Sindh Frontier district, the district magistrate considered that the large increase in reported offences against property was to a great extent due to thefts of cattle to replace the many that drowned in the floods that had inundated Sukkur district. Cattle were essential for agriculture but because of unsettled conditions in the country cattle-stealing was more prevalent than ever. The deputy inspector-general of police (IG) said this in his report:

> This form of crime does not give the police much work, as the owners of stolen cattle usually get their cattle back by compounding with the thieves and do not worry the police. At first sight it might appear to be a blot on the administration that the public are not protected against the ravages of the cattle thieves; but this is not so. The state of affairs that exists is really a reflection on the ethical conceptions of a large proportion of the landed gentry of the province. Cattle lifting is not considered to be an offence involving moral turpitude. An effort will shortly be made to strike at the principal organisers which will lead to considerable reduction in this form of crime. When cattle lifting is eventually stamped out, the police force will have to be considerably augmented as the bad characters will then have recourse to other forms of crime, such as highway robberies and burglaries, the victims of which will be much more vocal than the long-suffering cultivators of Sindh. (Ibid., p. 715).

In his report for the year 1934 the DIG attributed the increase in crime in the Upper Sindh Frontier district to general economic depression, restricted agricultural credit and consequent exhaustion of the *zamindar's* accumulated resources, and the partial failure of the *kharif* and *rabi* crops. He continued:

> In Sindh, the crime barometer used to rise and fall with the quality of the harvest, but nowadays the position is more complex, since the construction of the Lloyd Barrage most of the districts have an assured perennial water supply. But the development of the newly irrigated areas has led to a large influx of agricultural labourers, particularly from the Punjab, about whom the local police know nothing. The Punjab police have warned us against their criminals visiting Sindh in the guise of labourers and an effort is being made to check the antecedents of all newcomers in co-operation with the landowners. (Ibid., p. 715).

The population of Sindh was growing rapidly without any corresponding increase in the strength of the police.

The stubborn continuation of cattle theft was the subject of a notice by the District Superintendent of Police of Sukkur in the Administration Report for the year 1937. He said that *bhung* was still prevalent in the district and quoted Major Dunsterville, who had been magistrate of the Sukkur district some seventy years earlier:

> It is a distressing thought that justice or redress even in present times is rejected in favour of the quicker and more convenient system of *Bhung* and it is with some diffidence that I offer any suggestions regarding this problem. It is still an unsolved issue, and might receive the attention of social reform organizations after they have eradicated such vices as *rasai, lapo* and *cher.*

Also in the report for 1937, the rise in cognizable crime was notable in every district except Karachi. The Deputy Superintendent of Police (DSP) reported:

> The rise in cognizable crime may be due to a certain extent to the growing lack of respect for authority and to a realization on the part of persons with criminal tendencies that the arm of the Law is not as long as it used to be. In spite of the continuous abuse to which the police have been subjected, and the frequency of false or exaggerated charges against them, I have no reason to believe that the morale of the services has suffered to any appreciable extent. A sustained effort is being made by the superior officers of the force to give effect to the policy of Government in respect of the eradication of corruption and malpractice. We welcome criticism, but expect a fair deal from public speakers and the press. The most serious event of the year from the police point of view was the raid on the village of Kathiar, in the Dadu District, by a gang of Brahuis from the Kalat State. On their way back to Kalat they looted the camp of Mr Majumdar, Archaeological Superintendent, whom they killed. His murder was a great loss to archaeology.

The DSP remarked in the same report that, with the advent of a democratic government, the amount of assistance received by investigating officers from the zamindars steadily diminished. He says:

> Though this absence of public spirit is regrettable, I hope it will lead to a higher standard of investigation on the part of Police Station Officers. In those districts in which too much reliance was placed on the help of zamindars the investigation was apt to be slipshod and inadequate with the result that many cases ended in the acquittal of the guilty person.

6

Fifty Years of the Sindh Police
—An Overview

The birth of Pakistan raised new hopes and aspirations in the police. Unfortunately, the initial years after independence witnessed much political turmoil and, being the capital city, Karachi suffered most on account of unstable state institutions. It would not be wrong to say that the trigger-happy image which the Sindh police have today was acquired during the late 1950s, and subsequently when students from all over Pakistan started agitating for the restoration of democracy, those from Karachi being in the forefront. Prior to this, in the eleven years since independence, there had been a massive influx of population into Karachi—refugees from India, and migrant workers from upcountry who came to the city because of its booming industry and commerce. This sudden increase in population required a much expanded police force, but the local population had other opportunities of employment so they were not inclined to enlist. This resulted in large-scale recruitments from upcountry. In subsequent years, when this police force was pitted against the students of Karachi, and later its labour, in a period of turbulent political agitation, the gulf between the police and public was further widened, reaching its climax on the eve of 1964 elections. By this time, the police had become an effective tool of government in suppressing its political opponents. Karachi became a bastion of struggle for democracy, and since then has been regarded as a city where the opposition is always strong.

During the riots in 1972, the police came down with a heavy hand, resulting in a further widening of the gulf between the police and the public. This same period saw a sudden rise in the affluence of urban Pakistanis—a spillover of the oil boom in the Gulf—and a concurrent rise in corruption in government departments: this new-found affluence triggered a rat race for acquiring higher standards of living. Police stations became centres of corruption in a social milieu where corruption permeated all walks of life. The next round of police-public confrontation in Sindh came in 1977, during the PNA agitation, when the province—in particular Karachi—endured the wrath of state power delivered through the police, as it did again in 1983, during the MRD movement against General Ziaul Haq's martial law. It can thus be seen how police high-handedness and atrocities left deep scars on the psyche of Karachi's citizens, who were mostly at the receiving end.

In the wake of the war in Afghanistan, guns and drugs added a new dimension to the crime scene and subsequently to the law and order situation in Sindh. A series of ethnic riots in Karachi totally transformed the policing concept and traumatized the police-public relationship. Widespread ethnic riots and a large-scale armed struggle in certain areas of Karachi put the police on the defensive and seriously eroded state authority and the writ of law. By this time the population of Karachi alone was nearing the ten million mark and it was recognized that, in the circumstances, it was impossible to police Sindh with a force of merely 22,000 policemen. While trouble continued unabated, a massive police expansion programme was undertaken by the government to stem the tide of lawlessness. In less than ten years the strength of the Sindh police was increased by more than 150 per cent, i.e. from 22,000 to 67,000 men. But new recruitment had to be carried out in such a rush that the expanded police force became a liability instead of contributing positively to the maintenance of law and order. During this period approximately 50,000 policemen were recruited all over Sindh against a training capacity of one-third that number. Not only was the newly recruited police force ill-trained and ill-equipped, but the antecedents of a large number of recruits could not be verified—

on three separate occasions, approximately 9,000 recruits were inducted in a single year. Furthermore, financial constraints meant that government was unable to provide proportionate funds for housing, transport, and other essential operational facilities for the expanded police force.

Between 1980 and 1990 the province suffered immensely because of a sudden increase in the incidence of kidnapping for ransom—an offence which was not new to the area. It dates back to the era of Raja Dahir when pirates hijacked a boat carrying gifts for the Muslim caliph, along with the Muslim women and children who were on board. The piracy and kidnapping resulted in the invasion of Sindh by Mohammad Bin Qasim. However, it was during the period 1980–90 that the people of Sindh suffered most on account of kidnapping for ransom crime. The higher incidence of this was also due to the Sukkur jailbreak in 1986, when some notorious criminals escaped who later made the riverine areas of Ghotki, Sukkur, Khairpur, Jacobabad, Larkana, etc. their hideout.

The crime was at its peak in the early 1990s, almost 3,000 persons were kidnapped in the province during the first four months of 1992 alone. (Altaf Mujahid, '*Nawa-e-Waqt*', 27 August 1997).

The *sajjada nasheen* of Dargah Baiji was kidnapped along with sixteen of his disciples and brutally murdered in July 1992 by Hazuro Chacher. The passengers of a PIA van were kidnapped near Moenjodaro in 1995. Chinese engineers were kidnapped in Jacobabad district. A later and more well-known episode of this unending series was the kidnapping of Pir Mazharul Haq, a PPP leader, from the Super Highway in 1997. Dacoits like Paro Chandio, Nabi Chacher, Adam Jagirani, Kamal Faqeer, Sheru Rind, Nazar Narejo, Chakar, Fazal Bugti, etc. were very active during this period. Ultimately the government had to launch a massive operation with the help of the army—codenamed 'Blue Fox'—and since then incidence of this crime has shown a downward trend. However, it is worth noting that the gravity of the situation was recognized by the government and the need for a riverine police—popularly known as *'kacha'* area police—accepted. As a result, dozens of new police stations and police sub-divisions were sanctioned in the area and equipped with motor boats, APCs, etc., while the constabulary posted there was authorized to draw a special *kacha* allowance as an incentive.

Over the years the effectiveness of the *kacha* area police has been steadily diminishing: the equipment is wearing out for want of funds to carry out proper maintenance and most of the APCs and motor boats are awaiting repairs in police workshops. Another reason for this decline is that the police have still not been able to gain the confidence of the inhabitants of *kacha* area as is evidenced by their lack of support to the police. It is high time that the matter be given urgent attention and after carefully studying the crime pattern an effective strategy needs to be devised to curb the crime and prevent it from becoming as rampant as it was in the early 1990s.

Since the late 1980s, ethnic violence has posed yet another challenge for the Sindh police. The non-party general elections of 1985 led to the creation of new ethnic groups, the strongest of these being the Mohajir Qaumi Movement (MQM) headed by Altaf Husain. Sindhi-Mohajir clashes ensued but these were effectively checked by the police; anti-state activities by MQM outlaws were also foiled; and operations such as at Pukka Qila in Hyderabad, and similar ones in Sukkur and Karachi, were carried out in 1988 by the PPP regime to restore peace in Sindh. In the process, the MQM split, and a pro-establishment faction emerged as MQM Haqeeqi, headed by Aafaq Husain. Since then, occasional armed clashes between these two rival groups have endangered peace in different areas of Karachi and Hyderabad; disturbed areas of Karachi include Pak Colony, Orangi, Liaqatabad, Landhi, etc.

Non-party elections also gave rise to violent sectarianism. Some Deobandi factions of the *Jamiat Ulema-e-Islam* (JUI) and the Shia *Tehreek-e-Nifaz-e-Fiqah Jafaria* (TNFJ) transformed themselves into militant organizations such as *Sipah-e-Sahaba* and *Sipah-e-Mohammad*, and a serious problem of sectarian violence broke out in the province. The late 1990s witnessed a series of sectarian murders, particularly in Karachi, with 1999 being the worst year in this regard.

While housebreaking, house-robberies, highway dacoities, and kidnapping for ransom are the major problems for interior Sindh, carjacking is the major problem for Karachi. This does not mean that Karachi does not have incidences of house-robberies, but theft and snatching of vehicles—ten to fifteen every day—is the biggest worry for the people of the metropolis. The setting-up of an anti car-lifting cell in CIA under an SP was primarily to check this offence but so far no major success seems to have been achieved. There is a need to strengthen the check posts at the exit points of Karachi and to employ more technological and scientific aids to effectively check this crime.

As far as other achievements are concerned, the Sindh police are perhaps the only force in the world to have the distinction of carrying out a successful operation against aeroplane hijackers. On 24 May 1998, a PIA F-27 aircraft took off for Karachi from Gwadar but was hijacked en route by RAW (India's intelligence agency) agents who wanted to take it to India. The pilot landed at Hyderabad airport, deceiving the hijackers into believing that it was the Indian city of Bhuj in Gujarat state. The author was then SSP Hyderabad and headed the four-member team that was formed to handle the operation. The team introduced itself as Indian airport officials and, after seven-hour-long negotiations, the hijackers were arrested and the passengers and crew released unharmed. This event took place at a crucial time: Pakistan was all set to conduct its first nuclear test explosion at Chagai in Balochistan in four days' time. Had the hijacking been successful, Indian propaganda would have been able to stress that it showed that the people of Balochistan did not want a nuclear test, they wanted food and shelter instead. This operation was personally supervised by the IG Police, the Chief Secretary of Sindh, Commander 5 Corps, and the Chief Minister of Sindh; it was given wide coverage in the international media.

I have omitted discussion on the annual administration reports of the post-independence era because firstly, these were not available in the CPO Library and secondly, whatever information was available was not useful. The practice of writing annual administration reports is now only a formality of incorporating crime figures into a meaningless report of fifteen to twenty pages, with no attempt to analyse trends or make recommendations. Crime statistics for 1991–6 can be found at Appendices 7–15 (Statistical Branch, Central Police Office).

7

Improving the Police System

Although it is difficult to acknowledge bitter realities, there is no denying the fact that the police in Pakistan are one of the most ill-reputed departments in the country. Its poor reputation stems from its endemic corruption, its inefficiency, and its mistreatment of the general public. Much has already been written and said on the subject so, without entering into a discussion on the whys and wherefors of its poor image, I venture to offer some suggestions for its improvement.

1. Enhancing Pay and Allowances to Eradicate Corruption

I realize that the suggestion to enhance the pay and allowances of the police is not one that can be readily accepted in an underdeveloped country like Pakistan which is still striving to break free from the poverty trap, but we must not lose sight of the fact that the major factor in engendering corruption is the economic exploitation of the poor (which include government and police officials).

2. Improving Efficiency

Inefficiency normally results from the following:

(a) Lack of Training and Specialization
Although I do not see any major deficiency in the existing system of training, including the curricula at the Recruit Training

Centres, Police Training Colleges, and National Police Academy, these are some changes that would bring about increased efficiency. A key factor that impairs police efficiency is the absence of specialization within the service. Unfortunately, we have been blindly following the system inherited from the British. A police officer is expected to be a jack of all trades, but he proves to be master of none. Take the example of a head constable: while posted as a station clerk, he is required to be proficient in clerical duties, but by the time he has become fully conversant with his job, he is transferred as an investigating officer to a police station, where he is expected to be a good detective. After some time, he is posted to the traffic department, where it is essential for him to learn all the traffic rules and regulations. And there are yet other postings like the CIA, special branch, reserve police, etc. It is time to re-organize the police force into various branches which should be staffed by personnel who are specifically recruited and trained for each branch. Thus, an individual recruited for the traffic branch should be trained to perform traffic duties and should remain in that branch for the entire tenure of his service. Similarly, a clerical cadre should be separately raised (which could be integrated with the existing clerical cadre) to perform the duties of station clerk, lines clerk, etc. It is my personal experience that the staff currently working as station clerks (*moharrirs*) know very little about the job. The situation is not as bleak in the Punjab, but a general deterioration is noticeable even there. The detective and preventive branches should also be separated while the special branch, prosecution branch, and the reserve police have already been separated to a great extent. The process of specialization will definitely bring about a qualitative change in police efficiency.

(b) Lack of Supervision and Guidance

Lack of proper supervision and guidance are also major causes for the prevalent inefficiency. Every individual must be fully aware that he or she is answerable and accountable to a superior. The performance of the subordinate staff should be evaluated through a regular system of monthly inspections instead of the six-monthly inspections currently in vogue. To inculcate a healthy sense of competition, the professional performance of all officers should be graded on the basis of the monthly crime reports from their respective areas, with suitable rewards or commendation certificates given to those who do well and requiring improved performances from those who fare poorly. The supervisory role designated to the sub-divisional police officer, whether an ASP or a DSP, and the DIG has proved to be ineffective and requires to be redefined. These ranks must be made more effective. I do not tend to agree with the idea being floated nowadays that a police station should be headed by a DSP. It was the Karachi police that first initiated this proposal, during a briefing to the President on 6 January 1997. If this proposal were to be accepted, it would, in fact, further degrade the rank of a DSP. The experiment of upgrading the post of an SHO from a sub-inspector to an inspector has also not proved to be a success.

(c) Lack of Motivation
A commander must recognize that to successfully achieve any given task, the men under his command must be motivated and prepared to give of their best. An unwilling and demoralized worker, regardless of his intrinsic abilities, will never be fully committed and will deliver only a lackadaisical performance. It is essential that commanders at all levels make special efforts to motivate men and ensure that morale remains high. There are, of course, very many ways to do this, but a very basic requirement is for commanders to demonstrate an empathetic understanding of the grievances and personal problems of their men, and to take steps to alleviate them. Only when the welfare of the rank and file is accorded the priority it deserves will we be able to motivate them to work with commitment and dedication.

(d) Outdated Arms and Lack of Equipment and Transport
The Sindh police is deficient in modern arms, ammunition, wireless, transport, computers, etc and each police station and

police post should have its own transport and wireless sets, each picket detailed for patrolling or barricade duty should be similarly equipped. The use of information technology must now be expanded so that every police station is networked and provided access to specified levels of the police database. Old and outdated arms should be replaced with modern, automatic weapons. The use of armoured personnel carriers, night-vision binoculars, and bullet-proof jackets should be routine. Having served in both the provinces, I am of the view that the Sindh police has greater potential than the Punjab police and can perform well provided it is fully equipped and properly trained.

(e) Staffing

As far as understaffing is concerned, Sindh is fortunate not to be handicapped in this area, unlike the case in the Punjab and other provinces. The strength of the Sindh police, which was 13,300 in 1947, rose to 93,556 in 1997. In Sindh the ratio of strength to area is one constable for every 2.42 sq.km. against 4.05 sq.km. in the Punjab, 3.95 sq.km. in the NWFP, and 31.4 sq.km. in Balochistan. Similarly, the ratio of strength to population in Sindh is one constable for 327 persons, against 932 persons in the Punjab, 587 persons in the NWFP, and 392 persons in Balochistan. The ratio of strength to reported crime in Sindh is one constable for 0.72 reported cases, as against 3.86 cases in the Punjab, 4.30 cases in the NWFP, and 0.83 cases in Balochistan.

The following chart shows the comparative staffing of the four provinces.

One Constable for	Area (sq.km)	Persons	Reported Cases
Sindh	2.42	327	0.72
Punjab	4.05	932	3.86
NWFP	3.95	587	4.30
Balochistan	31.4	392	0.83

Province	Sindh	Punjab	NWFP	Balochistan
Total Area (sq.km.)	140,914	205,334	74,521	347,190
Population (1981 census)	19,028,666	47,292,441	11,061,328	4,332,376
Total Number of Crimes Reported (1996)	42,339	196,019	81,113	6,096
Total Number of Constables(Province)	69,822	67,966	25,097	11,053
Total Number of Constables in Police Districts*	58,156	50,726	18,854	7,349
	(21 districts)	(34 districts)	(23 districts)	(12 districts)

*This means strength deployed on active police duties in a police district excluding Reserve Police, Special Branch, Crimes Branch, training schools, CPO staff, etc.

A study of the chart below, showing the strength of Sindh police (all ranks) in the decades from 1940 to 1997, is instructive. It shows that there was a gradual increase until the mid-1980s, but then a sharp increase. This resolved the problem of understaffing but, because the induction was large and hurried, it resulted in adversely affecting the quality of manpower and the efficiency of the service.

Year	Strength	Year	Strength
1940	6,185	1980	29,564
1950	13,300	1985	39,287
1960	17,046	1990	60,509
1970	19,406	1997	93,556

To fill a large number of vacancies in both the lower and higher ranks, poor-quality manpower was inducted whose chief merit was political affiliation rather than ability. The result is that we occasionally find uniformed people involved in cases like dacoities, burglaries, rape, etc. While posted as SSP Sukkur, I had to terminate as many as sixty constables, eight head constables, two ASIs, and one SI within the short span of three months because of indiscipline and other charges. This type of surgical cleansing is essential to keep the force disciplined and on its toes.

3. Public Dealing

It is a common complaint that the lower ranks of the police are rude and overbearing in their dealings with the general public. This is a contentious issue, and much could be said on the subject, but there is no doubt that such accusations are frequently and publicly levelled.

The harsh and ill-mannered behaviour of the police has two causes. Firstly, the post of constable (and other lower ranks) is not viewed as being 'respectable' and thus it is mostly people from the lower middle class who volunteer for recruitment. Secondly, the required educational qualification for the post of constable is only matriculation, which does not provide adequate academic knowledge, only the rudimentary skills of reading and writing. Handicapped as they are with a social and cultural background that failed to groom them in higher standards of morality and character, and being barely literate, it would be unrealistic to expect police constables to conduct themselves with greater civility and propriety.

To bring about a qualitative change in the police, the minimum qualification for appointment to the post of constable should be Intermediate, and, in times, a bachelor's degree. Irrelevant restrictions like chest measurement etc. should be dispensed with—we reject a graduate candidate for the simple reason that his chest does not measure 33 to 34 ½ inches (a relic of colonial rule). Also, the rank of constable/head constable should be abolished and the lowest tier of the hierarchy should be ASI. Upgrading the post of constable (BS 5) to that of ASI (BS 9) would not have a major budgetary impact, but it would lend respectability to the force and attract young men and women from the upper middle class to join.

The general public comes into direct contact with the police at a police station, which they visit either to report a crime or to have their documents verified, e.g. passports, licences, etc. However, police stations do not have reception counters to receive visitors, nor responsible officials to attend to them. The unfortunate visitor therefore becomes a football shuttled between the SHO and the *moharrir* (station clerk) and, when he finally returns home unattended and unheard, one can understand why he curses the police for their inefficiency and callous attitude. It is important to correct this situation and make police stations more people-friendly. One of the ways to do this is to set up reception counters at each police station, manned by courteous and helpful clerks who attend to each visitor and direct him to the appropriate officer.

Traffic is another branch which, like the police station, plays an important role in forming the image of the police. After careful selection, only highly educated, disciplined, and courteous police officers should be posted to the traffic police. Roadside corruption should be effectively checked.

A positive change in the conduct of the police *vis-à-vis* the public it seeks to serve and protect can only come about slowly and gradually, and an overnight change should not be expected.

4. The Police in the Community

Effective community policing both enhances neighbourhood security and helps to alleviate the constant fear that one might become the next victim of some crime. This is achieved when the police, local government, and the community work closely together and combine their resources. All elements of society must join hands if we are to deal effectively with the unacceptable level of crime in our neighbourhoods.

In the same context, a national debate on restructuring the police continues at all levels. Issues such as de-politicizing the police and allowing control of the force to devolve in conformity with a democratic polity are all very relevant as these impact the strategy of orienting the police towards community service. The following measures to create a people-friendly police are recommended:

(a) As a first step, DIGs and SSPs should develop a community service programme based on the following:

   (i)   The police are a service, not a force. They can no longer act as the repressive arm of the government.
   (ii) The Sindh police must build a positive image of the service.
   (iii) All officers should learn to be sensitive to the aspirations of the various segments of society, especially the less privileged, the man in the street, women, children, etc.

(b) Police personnel should be courteous and polite when dealing with the public. They must learn to adopt a positive and helpful attitude towards the people who approach them, regardless of whether their problem concerns the police or not.

(c) Police officers must establish a comfortable and easy relationship with the media and be more open and forthcoming with such information as does not compromise ongoing investigations.

(d) Supervision at police stations and offices should be such that the emphasis is on discipline, cleanliness, and tidiness.

(e) The uniform, turn-out, and bearing of the force should be worthy of respect.

(f) Weekly character-building lectures for the staff should be organized at all police stations.

(g) The traffic police have a key role in building the image of the police. DIG Traffic should arrange short courses that bring about a positive change in the attitude and orientation of traffic constables, especially those manning road-crossings where they are the focus of attention of thousands of commuters.

(h) DIG Training should review the syllabi at all training institutions and incorporate subjects such as character-building and public relations, with emphasis on the need to change the orientation of the police.

5. Gender Sensitivity

This is another important issue. Management should work closely with those NGOs who have been asking that policewomen be given a better status and more conducive working conditions, and be guided by them in identifying ways to achieve this. Similarly, male police officers must be made more sensitive to gender issues. The Women's Action Forum could also be involved here.

The DIGs and SSPs should personally ensure that female victims are given full assistance and protected from the tyranny of the unfortunate social system, especially in the rural areas. Strengthening the women police, upgrading their facilities, and recruiting more women in the cadre must be undertaken on a priority basis.

6. Computerization

It is now essential that police personnel of all ranks be made computer literate. It will therefore be necessary to establish a computer training school which could also operate the police computer systems and prepare customized software for police functions.

7. Policing and the Media

Due importance must be given to the media as it is instrumental in creating the public's perception of the police. To establish a relationship of trust and confidence between the police and the community it is vital that complete and truthful information is shared with the public, especially concerning policies and police actions.

8

Overhauling the System of Criminal Justice

To improve the system of criminal justice, the following measures are recommended:

1. Judicial Inquiries instead of Police Investigations

When an offence is committed, it should be reported to the area magistrate or the judge instead of the police. The magistrate should then visit the crime scene, listen to the parties involved, and give his ruling there and then. In the present system, it is the police officer who visits the scene and starts the inquiry; the SHO or the investigating officer then acts like a judge; parties to the dispute are therefore required to prove their innocence or guilt twice: firstly to the police and then in court. Thus, a parallel judicial system comes into existence.

I believe the responsibility of determining the guilt or innocence of an accused should not rest with police because in our system of government, the police are under the direct or indirect control of politicians who have their own vested interests. The police are susceptible to political influence and often find it very difficult to administer justice. At the police station level, there should be a judge or a magistrate (along with assistants) who, on receipt of a complaint or a report of an offence, should immediately start the process of a judicial inquiry. There is no reason why a judge or magistrate should depend upon the police except in cases like blind murder (where culprits are unknown or unidentified), blind theft, or robbery, where investigation is actually required. For this purpose, a group of detective police officers, well-versed in detective techniques like photographing the crime scene, preserving fingerprints, chemical and ballistic examinations, etc., should be at the disposal of the judge/ magistrate. In our day-to-day working, in 70 per cent of cases the judge or magistrate would not require police detectives to investigate the case.

2. Revised Procedure for Recording an FIR

In the present system of criminal justice, a First Information Report (FIR) is accorded excessive importance. The weightage given to the FIR can be judged by the fact that some innocent people have been hanged simply because their names happened to be in the FIR; similarly, real culprits have been let off because an unfortunate complainant omitted to have their names recorded. In fact, an FIR is recorded at a very early stage of the investigation when the facts of the case are not very clear. Why such initial information is assigned so much sanctity is beyond comprehension.

In my scheme of things, the complaints or reports of offences should be filed on plain paper. The judge/magistrate should visit the scene of the offence and, after conducting a preliminary inquiry, should write a factual report in the register of crimes. This report should form the basis of the case and should be known as an Initial Factual Report (IFR). If an accused requires a copy of the IFR, this should be provided on his written request. The superior or appellate courts would give due consideration to the IFR before deciding appeals and bail petitions.

3. Decision of Cases through Summary Proceedings

On receipt of a complaint, the judge/magistrate should visit the scene of the offence, listen to all parties to the dispute, and, on the second or at most third hearing, decide the case by way of summary proceedings, without police investigations. Only complex cases would need to be referred to the police for further investigation. The verdict should be handed down within fourteen days because, as is said, justice delayed is justice denied. The appellate courts, however, would take as much time as was required to deliver a fair and just decision.

4. Detection and Prevention of Crime

My dream police station is headed by a magistrate or a judge, assisted by additional judges or magistrates, with a group of detective police officers at their disposal to conduct investigations where these are required. Ordinary and routine cases would be dealt with by the judges/magistrates without unnecessary and excessive police investigations.

For the prevention of crime, there would be designated and well-trained police officers to perform day/night patrolling, static picket duties, etc. They would be the actual crime fighters.

5. Internal Administration and Discipline

The supervision and discipline of both preventive and detective police would be dealt by the DSP at the sub-divisional level.

6. Induction of Judges or Magistrates

There are 354 police stations in Sindh and 604 in the Punjab. Initially, there should be at least one judge or magistrate at every police station where the crime rate is below 200 reported cases, with a pro rata increase in the number of judges corresponding to an increase in the number of cases. Presently there are not enough judicial magistrates to implement this scheme; new ones could be recruited from amongst those police officers who are law graduates and from those executive magistrates who are prepared to accept this new post. A fresh induction could also be made on the basis of a competitive examination held by the Public Service Commission. The number of magistrates will in any case have to be increased because the main bottleneck in the judicial system is the shortage of judges. Each judge is currently required to deal with no less than 1,500 to 2,000 cases per month, something which is humanly not possible. The result is that pendency is on the increase. Thus, to improve the system of criminal justice, an increase in the number of judges is a basic pre-requisite.

7. Amalgamation of Civil and Criminal Cases

In my proposed system, the judge/magistrate of a police station will be empowered to take cognizance of cases of a civil nature as well as criminal cases. I am confident that he will be able to deal with those cases far more effectively than at present. The existing system of dealing with civil cases is defective to the point of collapse. If A has to receive a certain amount of money from B, and B is not willing to pay him back, A is required to file a civil suit; this can take decades to settle. Almost 70 per cent of the applications filed with police officers are of a civil nature, although the police are not empowered to take cognizance of civil cases. People still do not want to go to the civil courts because they have no faith in the judicial system. It is quite clear that, in order to bring about a positive change in the system of criminal and civil justice, there is a need to introduce the proposed reforms.

Appendix 1
Organization Tree for the Sindh Police

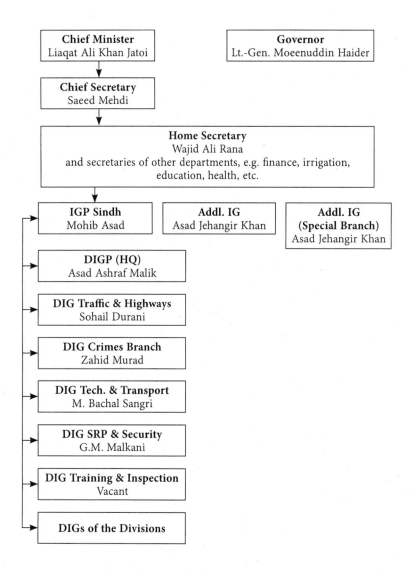

Appendix 2

Police Organization as on August 1947

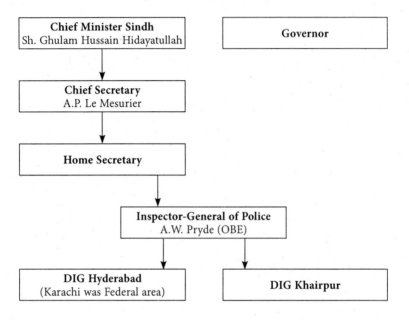

Appendix 3

Divisional and District Organization as on 14 August 1997

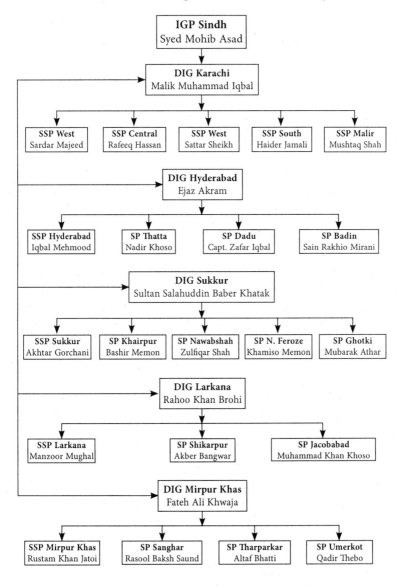

IGP Sindh
Syed Mohib Asad

DIG Karachi
Malik Muhammad Iqbal

SSP West	SSP Central	SSP West	SSP South	SSP Malir
Sardar Majeed	Rafeeq Hassan	Sattar Sheikh	Haider Jamali	Mushtaq Shah

DIG Hyderabad
Ejaz Akram

SSP Hyderabad	SP Thatta	SP Dadu	SP Badin
Iqbal Mehmood	Nadir Khoso	Capt. Zafar Iqbal	Sain Rakhio Mirani

DIG Sukkur
Sultan Salahuddin Baber Khatak

SSP Sukkur	SP Khairpur	SP Nawabshah	SP N. Feroze	SP Ghotki
Akhtar Gorchani	Bashir Memon	Zulfiqar Shah	Khamiso Memon	Mubarak Athar

DIG Larkana
Rahoo Khan Brohi

SSP Larkana	SP Shikarpur	SP Jacobabad
Manzoor Mughal	Akber Bangwar	Muhammad Khan Khoso

DIG Mirpur Khas
Fateh Ali Khwaja

SSP Mirpur Khas	SP Sanghar	SP Tharparkar	SP Umerkot
Rustam Khan Jatoi	Rasool Baksh Saund	Altaf Bhatti	Qadir Thebo

Appendix 4

Divisional and District Organization as on August 1947

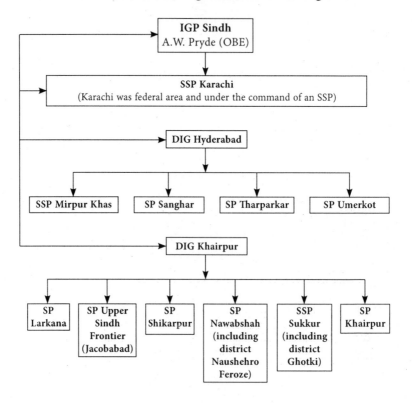

Appendix 5

An Example of District Organization as on 14 August 1997

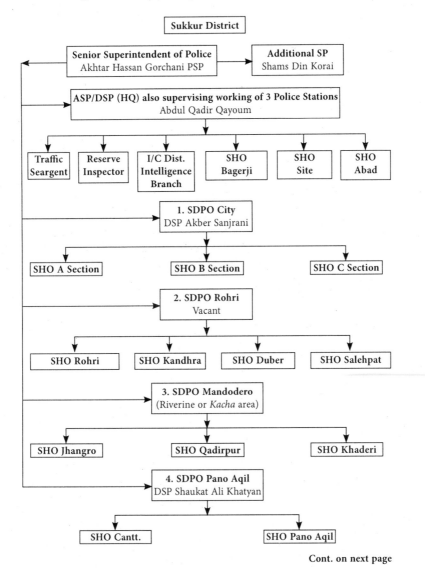

Sukkur District

Senior Superintendent of Police
Akhtar Hassan Gorchani PSP

Additional SP
Shams Din Korai

ASP/DSP (HQ) also supervising working of 3 Police Stations
Abdul Qadir Qayoum

| Traffic Seargent | Reserve Inspector | I/C Dist. Intelligence Branch | SHO Bagerji | SHO Site | SHO Abad |

1. SDPO City
DSP Akber Sanjrani

| SHO A Section | SHO B Section | SHO C Section |

2. SDPO Rohri
Vacant

| SHO Rohri | SHO Kandhra | SHO Duber | SHO Salehpat |

3. SDPO Mandodero
(Riverine or *Kacha* area)

| SHO Jhangro | SHO Qadirpur | SHO Khaderi |

4. SDPO Pano Aqil
DSP Shaukat Ali Khatyan

| SHO Cantt. | SHO Pano Aqil |

Cont. on next page

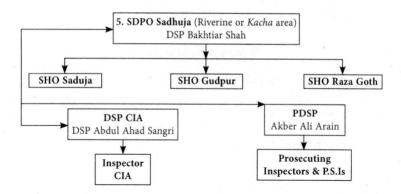

Appendix 6
Police Station Composition

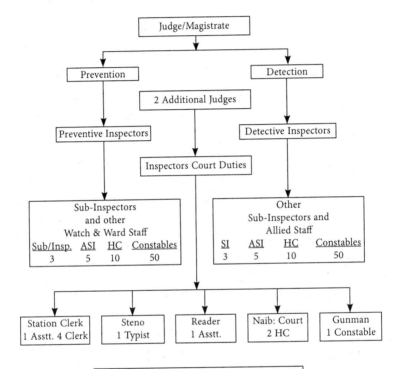

Judge/Magistrate

Prevention — Detection

2 Additional Judges

Preventive Inspectors — Detective Inspectors

Inspectors Court Duties

Sub-Inspectors and other Watch & Ward Staff				Other Sub-Inspectors and Allied Staff			
Sub/Insp.	ASI	HC	Constables	SI	ASI	HC	Constables
3	5	10	50	3	5	10	50

Station Clerk	Steno	Reader	Naib: Court	Gunman
1 Asstt. 4 Clerk	1 Typist	1 Asstt.	2 HC	1 Constable

2 Clerks to maintain daily diary of police station and to maintain certain crime registers

Process Service	Apprehension of accused
1 ASI, 2 HC, 8 Constables	1 SI, 2 ASI, 4 HC, 16 Constables

Total strength of an ordinary Police Station having less than 200 reported crime

Judge	Insp.	SI	ASI	HC	Constables	Steno	Asstt.	Clerks 6
3	3	7	13	28	125	1	2	(2 Senior, 4 Junior)

Appendix 7

Murder

S.No	Districts	1991	1992	1993	1994	1995	5-year average	1996
Karachi Range								
1.	East	208	155	137	354	386	248	134
2.	West	84	89	71	153	404	160.2	140
3.	South	94	77	82	133	153	107.8	89
4.	Central	74	58	52	223	531	187.6	89
5.	Malir	0	0	0	67	112	35.8	72
Total		460	379	342	930	1,586	739.4	524
Hyderabad Range								
6.	Hyderabad	145	117	70	82	112	105.2	75
7.	Dadu	153	118	76	102	95	108.8	83
8.	Thatta	41	42	33	33	46	39	33
9.	Badin	18	28	34	29	41	30	42
Total		357	305	213	246	294	283	233
Mirpurkhas Range								
10.	Mirpurkhas	54	36	35	21	23	33.8	26
11.	Sanghar	49	51	52	46	60	51.6	81
12.	Umerkot	-	-	10	15	14	7.8	24
13.	Thar (Mithi)	1	4	2	6	4	3.4	8
Total		104	91	99	88	101	96.6	139
Sukkur Range								
14.	Sukkur	192	151	87	65	52	109.4	86
15.	Khairpur	97	71	90	100	95	90.6	99
16.	Ghotki	-	-	30	106	72	41.6	79
17.	Nawabshah	87	61	28	49	48	54.6	49
18.	Naushehro Feroze	74	43	42	44	49	50.4	44
Total		450	326	277	364	316	346.6	357
Larkana Range								
19.	Larkana	227	184	169	214	204	199.6	202
20.	Jacobadad	168	151	152	171	177	163.8	169
21.	Shikarpur	95	96	96	99	105	98.2	110
Total		490	431	417	484	486	461.6	481
Grand Total		**1,861**	**1,532**	**1,348**	**2,112**	**2,783**	**1,927.2**	**1,734**

Appendix 8

Attempted Murders

S.No	Districts	1991	1992	1993	1994	1995	5-year average	1996
Karachi Range								
1.	East	335	262	233	360	307	299.4	210
2.	West	143	127	133	192	212	161.4	170
3.	South	218	202	148	213	270	210.2	191
4.	Central	129	100	112	212	230	156.6	93
5.	Malir	-	-	-	58	117	35	88
Total		825	691	626	1,035	1136	862.6	752
Hyderabad Range								
6.	Hyderabad	157	123	90	106	60	107.2	72
7.	Dadu	127	96	77	131	105	107.2	83
8.	Thatta	54	59	52	54	41	52	42
9.	Badin	62	43	42	42	36	45	49
Total		400	321	261	333	242	311.4	246
Mirpurkhas Range								
10.	Mirpurkhas	76	44	29	29	44	44.4	38
11.	Sanghar	58	50	40	57	59	52.8	57
12.	Umerkot	-	-	15	13	41	13.8	42
13.	Thar (Mithi)	4	4	7	2	6	4.6	5
Total		138	98	91	101	150	115.6	142
Sukkur Range								
14.	Sukkur	170	120	59	73	93	103	84
15.	Khairpur	64	66	81	106	117	86.8	99
16.	Ghotki	-	-	11	61	96	33.6	91
17.	Nawabshah	66	33	32	33	56	44	49
18.	Naushehro Feroze	61	40	31	44	47	44.6	35
Total		361	259	214	317	409	312	358
Larkana Range								
19.	Larkana	141	133	132	228	231	173	304
20.	Jacobadad	155	126	133	160	175	149.8	210
21.	Shikarpur	116	100	125	115	143	119.8	133
Total		412	359	390	503	549	442.6	647
Grand Total		2,136	1,728	1,582	2,289	2,486	2,044.2	2,145

66   APPENDIX

Appendix 9
Kidnapping for Ransom

S.No	Districts	1991	1992	1993	1994	1995	5-year average	1996
Karachi Range								
1.	East	17	11	3	4	7	8.4	6
2.	West	4	4	1	-	5	2.8	4
3.	South	3	3	2	6	5	3.8	6
4.	Central	76	74	83	53	51	67.4	70
5.	Malir	-	-	-	16	24	8	29
Total		100	92	89	79	92	90.4	115
Hyderabad Range								
6.	Hyderabad	76	44	12	13	12	31.4	16
7.	Dadu	96	86	12	6	4	40.8	4
8.	Thatta	1	2	1	-	-	0.8	7
9.	Badin	4	2	-	-	-	1.2	2
Total		177	134	25	19	16	74.2	29
Mirpurkhas Range								
10.	Mirpurkhas	5	2	11	1	1	4	-
11.	Sanghar	9	6	4	1	4	4.8	2
12.	Umerkot	-	-	-	-	-	0	-
13.	Thar (Mithi)	-	-	-	-	-	0	-
Total		14	8	15	2	5	8.8	2
Sukkur Range								
14.	Sukkur	51	22	4	4	2	16.6	5
15.	Khairpur	39	38	3	5	8	18.6	4
16.	Ghotki	-	-	3	10	9	4.4	4
17.	Nawabshah	51	43	29	6	2	26.2	-
18.	Naushehro Feroze	73	53	15	9	3	30.6	-
Total		214	156	54	34	24	96.4	13
Larkana Range								
19.	Larkana	39	57	3	6	4	21.8	3
20.	Jacobabad	7	9	-	1	5	4.4	14
21.	Shikarpur	9	8	2	3	3	5	4
Total		55	74	5	10	12	31.2	21
Grand Total		560	464	188	144	149	301	180

Appendix 10
Dacoity

S.No	Districts	1991	1992	1993	1994	1995	5-year average	1996
Karachi Range								
1.	East	33	28	56	34	44	39	49
2.	West	8	18	8	9	31	14.8	46
3.	South	23	17	19	35	33	25.4	50
4.	Central	39	37	63	73	86	59.6	134
5.	Malir	-	-	-	17	23	8	33
Total		103	100	146	168	217	146.8	312
Hyderabad Range								
6.	Hyderabad	15	27	16	21	17	19.2	24
7.	Dadu	34	14	4	19	7	15.6	13
8.	Thatta	3	2	2	5	4	3.2	5
9.	Badin	1	1	3	-	-	1	-
Total		53	44	25	45	28	39	42
Mirpurkhas Range								
10.	Mirpurkhas	-	1	5	1	5	2.4	2
11.	Sanghar	7	6	5	4	4	5.2	2
12.	Umerkot	-	-	-	-	4	0.8	2
13.	Thar (Mithi	-	-	-	-	1	0.2	-
Total		7	7	10	5	14	8.6	6
Sukkur Range								
14.	Sukkur	31	27	12	22	23	23	41
15.	Khairpur	24	10	21	28	33	23.2	26
16.	Ghotki	-	-	2	10	19	6.2	9
17.	Nawabshah	-	3	2	2	3	2	5
18.	Naushehro Feroze	16	5	18	13	3	11	9
Total		71	45	55	75	81	65.4	90
Larkana Range								
19.	Larkana	15	24	22	33	45	27.8	41
20.	Jacobabad	7	13	11	9	19	11.8	35
21.	Shikarpur	15	10	10	11	6	10.4	25
Total		37	47	43	53	70	50	101
Grand Total		271	243	279	346	410	309.8	551

Appendix 11
Robbery

S.No	Districts	1991	1992	1993	1994	1995	5-year average	1996
Karachi Range								
1.	East	152	121	168	139	107	137.4	231
2.	West	40	53	50	39	84	53.2	167
3.	South	93	99	122	212	326	170.4	518
4.	Central	72	66	270	119	153	136	373
5.	Malir	-	-	-	27	34	12.2	85
Total		357	339	610	536	704	509.2	1,374
Hyderabad Range								
7.	Hyderabad	244	242	158	183	178	201	96
8.	Dadu	58	41	39	47	46	46.2	21
9.	Thatta	24	18	16	22	23	20.6	27
10.	Badin	15	6	11	8	20	12	11
Total		341	307	224	260	267	279.8	155
Mirpurkhas Range								
11.	Mirpurkhas	21	7	9	8	15	12	24
12.	Sanghar	21	14	11	11	13	14	17
13.	Umerkot	-	-	1	1	2	0.8	3
14.	Thar (Mithi)	-	-	1	2	1	0.8	-
Total		42	21	22	22	31	27.6	44
Sukkur Range								
15.	Sukkur	78	44	58	60	47	57.4	55
16.	Khairpur	37	17	21	27	34	27.2	45
17.	Ghotki	-	-	7	8	24	7.8	12
18.	Nawabshah	21	10	7	5	20	12.6	29
19.	Naushehro Feroze	15	9	38	17	32	22.2	9
Total		151	80	131	117	157	127.2	150
Larkana Range								
20.	Larkana	52	45	67	118	144	85.2	103
21.	Jacobabad	36	23	28	18	22	25.4	32
22.	Shikarpur	27	24	33	37	23	28.8	28
Total		115	92	128	173	189	139.4	163
Grand Total		1,006	839	1,115	1,108	1,348	1,083.2	1,886

Appendix 12
Burglary

S.No	Districts	1991	1992	1993	1994	1995	5-year average	1996
Karachi Range								
1.	East	427	442	395	188	176	325.6	141
2.	West	151	151	162	113	102	135.8	117
3.	South	224	227	182	192	105	186	131
4.	Central	213	224	325	225	195	236.4	200
5.	Malir	-	-	-	62	49	22.2	59
Total		1,015	1,044	1,064	780	627	906	648
Hyderabad Range								
6.	Hyderabad	176	172	189	253	159	189.8	130
7.	Dadu	74	58	56	104	51	68.6	57
8.	Thatta	24	22	19	43	26	26.8	29
9.	Badin	21	21	26	28	39	27	31
Total		295	273	290	428	275	312.2	247
Mirpurkhas Range								
10.	Mirpurkhas	28	31	35	21	31	29.2	40
11.	Sanghar	31	23	46	44	38	36.4	31
12.	Umerkot	-	-	11	8	12	6.2	17
13.	Thar (Mithi)	3	2	1	1	3	2	2
Total		62	56	93	74	84	73.8	90
Sukkur Range								
14.	Sukkur	108	109	99	80	75	94.2	95
15.	Khairpur	33	25	18	21	24	24.2	24
16.	Ghotki	-	-	7	39	43	17.8	25
17.	Nawabshah	44	45	43	27	12	34.2	28
18.	Naushehro Feroze	23	20	23	31	39	27.2	59
Total		208	199	190	198	193	197.6	231
Larkana Range								
19.	Larkana	37	53	103	83	51	65.4	79
20.	Jacobabad	42	42	76	52	86	59.6	126
21.	Shikarpur	53	26	30	44	40	38.6	72
Total		132	121	209	179	177	163.6	277
Grand Total		1,712	1,693	1,846	1,659	1,356	1,653.2	1,493

Appendix 13

Motorcycle Theft/Snatching

S.No	Districts	1991	1992	1993	1994	1995	5-year average	1996
Karachi Range								
1.	East	-	567	864	845	913	637.8	972
2.	West	-	126	154	184	314	155.6	328
3.	South	-	645	878	1,282	1,631	887.2	1,421
4.	Central	-	361	839	759	1,215	634.8	1,107
5.	Malir	-	-	-	173	166	67.8	134
Total		0	1,699	2,735	3,243	4,239	2,383.2	3,962
Hyderabad Range								
6.	Hyderabad	-	66	73	83	79	60.2	73
7.	Dadu	-	10	16	19	16	12.2	20
8.	Thatta	-	7	7	10	10	6.8	6
9.	Badin	-	2	4	9	3	3.6	6
Total		0	85	100	121	108	82.8	105
Mirpurkhas Range								
10.	Mirpurkhas	-	5	7	21	23	11.2	33
11.	Sanghar	-	6	22	16	18	12.4	25
12.	Umerkot	-	-	2	4	4	2	10
13.	Thar (Mithi)	-	-	-	-	3	0.6	-
Total		0	11	31	41	48	26.2	68
Sukkur Range								
14.	Sukkur	-	40	25	38	52	31	28
15.	Khairpur	-	6	21	19	12	11.6	6
16.	Ghotki	-	-	-	5	14	3.8	24
17.	Nawabshah	-	23	24	20	31	19.6	13
18.	Naushehro Feroze	-	1	2	3	3	1.8	7
Total		0	70	72	85	112	67.8	78
Larkana Range								
19.	Larkana	-	18	25	37	41	24.2	62
20.	Jacobabad	-	-	4	32	29	13	29
21.	Shikarpur	-	2	8	5	21	7.2	32
Total		0	20	37	74	91	44.4	123
Grand Total		0	1,885	2,975	3,564	4,598	2,604.4	4,336

Glossary

Barkandazes	A special force set up to protect the treasuries and escort the consignment of treasuries
Bhung	blackmail paid for redeeming a stolen animal (now used for kidnapped persons)
Cher	System of forced labour
Hadd	Limitations i.e. criminal law punishments
Iqleem	province
Jagirdar/Zamindar	landlord
Kardar	district head
Kharif	autum crop
Kotwal	city police chief
Lapo	allowance given to reapers, field watchmen, and others. An allowance or fixed perquisite; a kind of perquisite
Mamlatdar/Tehsildar	subdivsional officer
Munsif	judge or magistrate
nakabandi	snap checking
Parganah	(*kiltas + qasbahs*) group of villages
Qazi-e-quzzat	Chief Justice
Rabi	spring harvest; grain produced in the spring
Rasai	The system of supplying necessities gratis or at a nominal price to officials and their establishments while touring
Sarkar	district
Shiqadar-e-Shiqadaran	head of district administration
Shiq	Subdivision of a district
Sajjada-nashin	spiritual leader

Subedar/nazim	overseer
Taluka/Tehsil	subdivision
Zabta-e-faujdari	code of criminal procedure

REFERENCES

Abbott, J. *Sind, a reinterpretation*, 1977.

Al-Mawardi, Abu al-Hasan Ali. *Al-Ahkam al-Sultania w'al-Wilayat al-Diniyya.*

Burton, Richard Francis. *Sindbar*, 1877.

Elliot, Henry. *The History of India as Told by Its Own Historians.*

Mujahid, Altaf. Article in *Nawa-e-Waqt*, 27 August 1997.

Nabi, Aftab. *Notes.*

Nadvi, Syed Suleman. *Tareekh-e-Hind.*

Rizvi, N.A. *Our Police Heritage.*

Siraj, Shamsi. *Tareekh-e-Sindh.*

Sorely, Herbert T. *The Sind Gazetteer.*

INDEX

Chakar, 40
Chandio, Paro, 40
Charlemagne, 4
Cher, 36
Chinese, 8, 40
Chowkis, 12
CIA, 42, 44
Civil Cases, 56
Civil Suit, 56
Code of Criminal Procedure, 22, 26
Commissioner of Sindh, 21
Community, 50
Computerization, 52
Corruption, 45
Criminal Justice, 53, 56
Curzon Police Commission, 21
Cyrus, 8

D

Dadu District, 36
Dahir, Raja, 40
Dara, 8
Dargah Baiji, 40
Darius, 8
Day/night patrolling, 55
Delhi, 10, 13
Deobandi, 41
Deputy Inspector-General (DIG), 23,
    32, 35, 46, 51; (crimes), 24;
    (headquarter), 24; (SRP &
    Security), 26; (traffic), 24; T&I
    (training and inspection), 24; T&T
    (technical and transportation), 24
Deputy Superintendent (DSP), 23-7,
    36, 46
District Intelligence Branch (DIB),
    27
District Police Headquarters, 22
drabeen, 7
Drugs, 39
Durani, Sohail, 57

E

Efficiency, 45
ehdaas, 6
Elliot, Sir Henry, 11
England, 4
Equipment and Transport, 46

F

Faqeer, Kamal, 40
Faujdar, 9, 12, 15
Faujdari adawlat, 16
Female Victims, 52
First Information Report (FIR), 26,
    54
France, 4, 5
Frank-pledge, 4
Frontier, 31

G

Gender Sensitivity, 52
Ghauri, Mohammad, 8
Ghotki, 40
Grand Trunk Road, 9
Greek, 8
Gujarat, 1, 42
Gulf, 39
Guns, 39
Gupta dynasty, 8
Gwadar, 42

H

hadd, 7
Haq, General Ziaul, 39
Haq, Pir Mazharul, 40
Hassan, Rafeeq, 59
Hazrat Abu Bakar (RA), 6
Hazrat Ali (RA), 6
Hazrat Umar (RA), 6
Hidayatullah, Sh. Ghulam Hussain,
    58